EXTREME GREENS

UNDERSTANDING SEAWEEDS

cooking * foraging * cosmetics

Sally McKenna

Estragon Press

First published in 2013 by Estragon Press
Durrus, County Cork, Ireland

ISBN 9781906927196

PRINTED IN SPAIN BY GRAPHYCEMS

Photographs: page 12 by Megan Clancy, page 94 by Anthony Dalton and page 191 by John McKenna. All other photographs by Sally McKenna.

Editor Judith Casey

Illustrations by Connie McKenna.

Note that wild food can be dangerous. Do not eat anything from the wild unless you know what you are eating, and understand the environment in which it grows.

for John

with special thanks and love to Connie, Sam and PJ

Thanks to Jim and Maria Kennedy, with whom I first embarked on this journey. Also to my family, my mother Margie and my brother Chris and his wife Alex. Thanks to seaweed-loving friends who helped, especially Freddie O'Mahony for sharing so much – including the best place locally to collect seaweed. Thanks to Ger Talty for The Knowledge, to Jasper Winn for sending me sea flowers, to Carmel Somers for the inspiration and shared seaweed sessions. I'm also grateful for the books and advice given to me by fellow food blogger and chef Pat McLarnon. Thanks particularly to Paul Nielan and Chris Carroll from Gill & Macmillan, for all the advice and guidance. Also to our wonderful editor, Judith Casey, who is so brilliant with cookery terms and phrases, and to Caroline Hennessy for her advice, which came at just the right time. Warm thanks to Susan Steele, Darina Allen and Joanna Blythman, the first people to see the book, for their enthusiasm just when pre-publishing doubt began to creep in. Thanks to Hugh Stancliffe and all at GraphyCems for their kindness and diligence. As always, thank you to Frank McKevitt, Edwina Murray and Dr Denis Cotter. And also to our inspirational food friends Bridget Healy, Caitlin Ruth and Enrico Fantasia.
And my final thanks to the person who is crucial in almost every element of all our lives, Eve Clancy.

Foreword

Imagine being offered plentiful free food. Imagine if this free food was packed with health promoting minerals, nutrients and anti oxidants which could help you to live longer and fight disease, help you to lose weight, and give shiny healthy skin and hair.

Imagine a natural, sustainable free food which is also proven to confer health benefits on your pets, livestock and chickens. A free food that will make the vegetables in your garden germinate faster and be more resistant and give better yields. Sally McKenna offers you this free and plentiful food through this book.

My name is Susan Steele, I was inspired by the oceans at the age of three and I have dedicated my life to the seas ever since, working as a marine biologist, a seafood innovator and currently heading the Sea Fisheries Protection Authority.

You have a number of choices on how to use this superb work by Sally McKenna. You can choose to use it as a coffee table book and admire the skilled photography and the recipes but not put it to use. You can choose to try some of the recipes using dried seaweeds. Or you can choose to use the book to open the doors to a wondrous new world and to amazing adventures which have inspired Sally McKenna in writing the book.

I believe that there is nowhere as relaxing as by a shore on low tide surrounded by the greens, browns and reds of seaweed. I believe that there is nothing as delicious as many of the recipes using seaweed and I believe that there is nothing as healthy as eating seaweed.

Enjoy this book, embrace the new ideas and explore a part of natural Ireland that you may not have appreciated fully.

Dr Susan Steele,
PhD, MBA, MEd
Executive Board Member
Sea Fisheries Protection Authority

Contents

introduction

We often give credit to our weather for colouring our fields in forty shades of green and blessing our beef and our butter with a deliciousness above any other.

We could also voice this assertion for our seaweed, and perhaps we still might.

Ireland's latitude and position makes it hospitable to marine life that loves both warm and cold water. Our westerly coastline is buffered by intense wave action that is enjoyed by both surfers, and sea vegetables.

Our sloping sea bed and the rocky substratum beneath it, the bays and inlets and the exposed rock faces, all offer different aspects and attractions to different types of seaweed. It's a good place to live.

So, come the March equinox and, if you go down to our rocky shores, your breath will be taken away by an abundance of life. Rich and diverse, and beautiful.

I first entered this world on a kayak. My craft took me to secret places where the water glowed a phthalo green-blue and the rock walls were lined with spicy pepper dulse above the waterline, and purple carrageen below the waterline that sparkled with vivid blue oxygen bubbles. I wanted to know more.

Before long, my kayaking role in Atlantic Sea Kayaking – where I work now and again – changed from being a trainee instructor to a foraging guide. And, in revealing this secret world to others, I began to learn more about how to understand seaweed myself.

It was a love of the seaweed environment that started me on this path, and this soon turned to a love of seaweed itself. As I studied it, I began to learn more about the tides, about the universe, about the historical context in which it was eaten. How it was used as a fertiliser, a medicine and a food.

I began to understand that what seaweed could famously do for plants, ie make them grow tall and strong, it could also do for my children. And also for my fifty-year-old self and my husband.

04-13
10 13

Seaweed has been a part of the Irish diet going right back to prehistoric times. Its use in cooking was described in fifth-century monastic writings. In pre-famine days the order of work for the woman of the house was said to be - 1. potatoes; 2. children (yes! in that order) and 3. seaweed: *Prátaí; Páiste; Feamainn.* Seaweed was right up there with the spuds and the kids, because its value to the household was intimately understood.

Nowadays research into seaweed has shown us scientifically what our forebears understood through experience. Seaweed is a superfood that can regulate metabolism, and with it our energy levels; it cleanses the blood, and stimulates our immune system.

Seaweed has both prebiotics and probiotics, and helps calm the digestive tract. It protects against bacterial and viral infection, and brings with it a punch of natural antibiotics. It maintains a healthy cellular function both within the body and on the skin, where it also protects and soothes. Even just taking a bath in seaweed brings all these benefits. Eating it even more so.

People often ask me how they can get children to eat seaweed, and the answer can be very simple. Seaweed in a powdered form can take on the flavour of anything you put it with, so a tablespoon of dilisk in a casserole, or even a cake, will not be taste-detected by a fussy child.

The benefits of seaweed are long term, and that's how they should be considered. The secret is to take small amounts, regularly.

The seaweed recipes in this book are for dishes that benefit from the addition of seaweed in a natural, logical way. Sometimes the seaweed is highlighted in the recipe, sometimes it plays a background role.

The recipes here are simple. My aim with these recipes is to help develop an understanding of what the different plants are good for. I would hope that the book can then be used as a stepping stone by anyone wanting to bring seaweed into their diet. An understanding of how it grows and tastes, I hope, will allow you to create your own recipes, and give you confidence to add it to your own favourite foods, and thereby enjoy the blessing of this wonderful ingredient.

Sally McKenna, Durrus, June 2013

wild seaweed

It is at the edge of nature that we find the greatest biodiversity. The edge: where two habitats combine – forest and meadow, road and pasture – is a place to find distinct flora.

Where land and sea meet is home to algae, or seaweed, possibly the oldest form of life on our planet and arguably the most bounteous.

identifying seaweed

Seaweeds are usefully divided into only three categories: green, red and brown. Sun-soaked green seaweeds are found on the upper shore, red seaweeds in the lower shore, and brown seaweeds are sandwiched in between them, with the large kelps in the sub tidal zone, and the wracks in the middle zone.

All play their part in the marine environment. Green algae provides shelter for the many sea creatures who eat and live at that level. Red algae has the most applications for human industry, from gelatins to cosmetics, and brown algae is the largest group, growing in huge forests, and is the main source of seaweed fertilizer.

There is an old Irish phrase: **Prátaí; Páiste; Feamainn** *– potatoes; children; seaweed. This was the order of care for the woman of the house in pre-famine times.*

harvesting seaweed

The majority of seaweeds are harvested between St Patrick's Day and late autumn, but this is often linked to the fact that it is easier to harvest in warm weather, rather than the seaweed being at its prime. There are plenty of seaweeds growing nicely through the winter months, with pepper dulse, perhaps, the finest winter treat.

March is possibly the best month to pick seaweed if you want to store it. This is generally before the plants begin to fruit. During high summer, for example, carrageen gets stiff and hairy, and many of the red seaweeds turn green as they become fertile.

A good tip, from seaweed harvester Ger Talty of Wild Irish Sea Veg, is to watch the periwinkles as they feed on the kelp. They will find the area that is richest in nutritients. When they reach the end of the frond, the plant is ready to spawn, and it is now time to stop picking.

channelled wrack

Channelled wrack always grows at the top of the tide line, in the intertidal "splash" zone. Its fronds form channels with which to catch the splashes. That is how it gets its name. In culinary terms, it bears a similarity to the Japanese seaweed called *hijiki*, and you can substitute it in *hijiki* recipes.

The botanical name for channelled wrack is *pelvetia canaliculata.* Its name in Irish is *dulamán* in County Clare, and *caisíneach* on the Aran Islands and in Connemara. One of its common names is *cow-tang.*

The smallest of all the wracks, channelled wrack attaches itself to the upper rocks. It has forked fronds that appear to flower for a good part of the summer, when it turns from its usual darker brown to a mustard yellow colour. The "flowers" are in fact the fruiting tips.

Channelled wrack is good in stir fries and salads and can be used in recipes in place of chopped sea spaghetti. It is, in fact, the most palatable of all the wracks, and because it is easily accessible, it's a versatile friend to the seaweed cook.

This is a seaweed that is especially rich in selenium and vitamin C.

Channelled wrack gives an excellent indication of the top of the tide mark – never pitch your tent or leave your shoes below the channelled wrack line.

the seaweeds

the wracks

At first one can get confused, looking at all the wracks that grow abundantly in the middle tide, but after a while you realise they are quite distinctive. Spiral wrack is at the top, literally twisting its leaves into a spiral. Then bladderwrack with its poppable air pockets, always arranged in pairs, and its characterful common name: *swine-tang*. Then the bulbous knotted wrack, aka egg wrack, which attracts its very own symbiotic fluff – a seaweed called *polysiphonia lanosa*, that always attaches itself to this species. This wrack grows an "egg" each year, so you can always tell how old it is.

Whilst channelled wrack marks the full reach of the high tide and forest kelp marks the depth of the spring lows, then serrated wrack records the level of the low tide mark of the neap tide and is a seaweed that is covered by water for fully half of the tidal cycle.

You can see how serrated wrack gets its common names: *serrated; toothed; saw wrack*. Its other distinctive features are a central rib, and the oil-rich pimples from the mature plant get more pronounced at the end of the season. The botanical name for serrated wrack is *fucus serratus*, and that's a name you will see listed on the contents of seaweed baths and in other cosmetic products.

Bladderwrack, whose bubbles we all so much enjoy popping, is very high in iodine, and is used medicinally to stimulate the thyroid, and consequently boost metabolism. It is also used for rheumatism, where it is made into an external application for inflamed joints.

pepper dulse

The tiniest of all the regularly eaten seaweeds, pepper dulse, may be small, but it's strongly built to resist wave attack. Its rounded fronds protect it from the worst of the pummelling sea action, and this distinctive sea vegetable is easily collected from rocks in the intertidal zone.

Best harvested carefully with scissors, pepper dulse is credited with being called no less than the truffle of the sea. Its flavour is a somewhat startling mixture of salt, pepper and a distinct fishiness. Chefs call for it to be dried and powdered, after which it makes an exceptional condiment. The botanical name for pepper dulse is *osmundea pinnatifida*.

The intense taste of pepper dulse dominates in the way garlic might. If you mix it with other seaweeds, all you will taste is the pepper dulse. So use it on its own.

So far there has only been a murmur about pepper dulse being commercially harvested. It requires careful picking, and if you aren't careful a lot of gritty sand can find its way into the bag too.

Dried and ground to a powder, pepper dulse is delicious in fish cakes, or for seasoning raw fish preparations. It also works as a substitute for black pepper.

Pepper dulse is best in winter, in all its purple glory. During the summer it can turn quite green in colour, with a slight diminishment of flavour.

the seaweeds

sea grass

Sea grass is a delicious summer annual that is sometimes marketed as Atlantic *spirulina*. Actually, it is technically neither a sea grass, nor a spirulina, but these rather more romantic names have come into common usage, possibly because its proper common name is gut weed (Latin *enteromorpha intestinalis*). The reason for this proper name is obvious when you see the plant floating in water: its shoots are made up of intestine-shaped tubes, full of the oxygen that has been expired by the plant.

I think, given that this is a recipe book, I'll not use the term gut weed, or *enteromorpha intestinalis*, but follow common practice and call it sea grass instead.

You must be careful when harvesting this seaweed, because it also enjoys brackish water and can sometimes flourish in polluted streams.

When you find it in abundance, check the area around you and try to work out where the water source is coming from. If it comes from suspicious looking drainage, leave well alone.

But sea grass also flourishes in clean sheltered bays and is one of the most useful of all sea vegetables.

Best of all, it keeps its distinctive taste in even the hottest baking. Don't be fooled by its light green promise of mildness, this is no featherweight, but rather an agrestic, flavourful seaweed that works well in seaweed butter, in flavoured breads, and whisked into smoothies.

the seaweeds

nori

Nori, laver, sloke, *sleabhac* - this is a jewel amongst sea vegetables. Prized in laverbread, essential in sushi, the sweet mellow taste and salty depth of flavour makes nori the most sought after seaweed in cooking. Nori is rich in the flavour-giving glutamates that cause our umami receptors to tingle.

Nori as we normally buy it - the square, slightly crispy palette for sushi-making - is nori that has been toasted and processed. Wild nori bears no resemblance. In fact the thing wild nori bears the most resemblance to is an abandoned black refuse sack, melted onto the rock by the sun. This is not a very promising plant when you find it, often coated in sand, on beaches or against steep exposed rock faces. But when cleaned and dried, the flavour is everything you want from a seaweed.

American botanist Cynthia T D Trowbridge (co-author of *The Biology of Rocky Shores*) described nori as "the dandelion of the sea" due to its habit of finding nooks and crannies in which to grow. There are many species, some winter growing, some summer. It's a seaweed that enjoys a bit of wave action, but also loves warm rocks buried in sand, from which it is most accessible.

The botanical name is *porphyra*, and *p. linearis*, which grows in winter, is said to be the most flavourful. *P. umbilicalis* gets its name from its central point of attachment.

As well as its application in sushi, nori is famous for being the chief ingredient in laverbread, when it is first boiled for up to ten hours to make it soft enough to purée.

the seaweeds

sea lettuce

Sea lettuce is a plant that is enjoyed by the sea hare, but this hare is no bunny, and sea lettuce is no salad leaf. The sea hare is actually a type of slug, and sea lettuce is a marine green algae with a strong, sea-salty, tang.

The leaves of sea lettuce grow rapidly from a perennial holdfast, in some areas arriving in a green tidal bloom that can be a coastal nuisance, decomposing with such an unpleasant stench that it needs tractors to clear it from tourist amenities.

Perhaps the best thing to do is to eat it.

The botanical name for sea lettuce is *ulva* and, like sea grass, the *ulva* species lives happily in brackish water, so be careful to make sure that you have sea lettuce from clean waters, at which point it is a fantastic plant for eating. It is also known as green laver and the Irish name is *glasán*.

One of the best things to do with sea vegetables is to enjoy their colours in a mélange, or seaweed salad. A flavoured butter, for example, that uses sea lettuce for green, dilisk for red, kelp for brown, and a little yellow lemon zest to lighten both the taste and colour, is one of the prettiest preparations.

Sea lettuce is a very rich source of iron, and is almost always eaten raw.

the seaweeds
carrageen

A funny thing happened to carrageen. It got posh. Whilst other seaweeds were derided as poor man's food, carrageen made it to the dessert trolley of smart country houses. A wobbly pudding, made from its jelly, was served in dainty dishes and partnered by gentrified fruit such as gooseberries. It was made into warm drinks and served in glasses with brandy and slices of lemon. It appeared on restaurant menus, moulded into elaborate seafood mousses. It even got posh names: *mousse d'Irlande*, Irish moss.

Possibly because it was so posh, somewhere along the line it was decided that carrageen should be bleached. If you ask seaweed gatherers why, they raise their eyes to heaven. There is no need for it. If anything, it detracts from the health benefits. But apparently people won't buy purple carrageen.

But there is yet another magical element to carrageen, and you can only witness this by wading through rock pools and seeking out the plant when it is submerged in seawater. In the wild, carrageen is lit up by an iridescence that appears as blue flashes of light. So powerful are the flashes that you can even capture them on film. These flashes are pure oxygen, which is released by the plant as it photosynthesises.

Carrageen aka *chondrus crispus,* aka E407, is used as a stabilizer, texturizer and emulsifier in everything from ice cream to infant formula.

On the shore it can be confused with another seaweed, *Mastocarpus*, but both produce *carageenan*, the gel that makes this plant so valuable.

the seaweeds

dilisk

Dilisk is probably the most accessible of the North Atlantic seaweeds. Used in cooking, it is often associated with humble, homely foods. Scones, soda bread, sandwiches, spuds: these are all foods that have been paired with this much-loved sea vegetable.

Coastal communities still talk of dilisk being eaten, like crisps, from a bag. It was even a snack that was taken to school in recent folk memory, in the days before cheese strings.

The only controversial thing about dilisk is its name. Is it dilisk or dulse? It tends to be one or the other in the minds of those who eat it. Its Irish name is *duileasc*, which sounds like a mixture of the two, and probably explains the confusion. Its botanical name is *palmaria palmata*, which derives from palm (*palma*) due to its resemblance to the human hand.

There is another name, *creathnach*, but this name is given to a second, smaller plant. This is shell dulse (shell dilisk?) a related plant that grows alongside seed mussel shells.

Dilisk is high in protein (up to 35%) as well as minerals and vitamins. It contains all the trace elements needed by humans, making it useful as both a food and a medicine.

It grows at the lower reaches of the tide, often growing as an *epiphyte* on the stipes of brown kelp.

sea spaghetti

Sea Spaghetti needs no description: its name describes everything you need to know. Also called *spaghetti de mer*, thongweed, sea thong, and button weed, it grows from a button-shaped perennial base, with a frond that grows annually. The only thing you could mistake it for is bootlace weed (*chorda filum*), which has the lovely alternative name of Mermaid's Tresses. The fronds of bootlace weed don't divide, or indeed grow from the distinctive button base.

Sea spaghetti (*Himanthalia elongata*) loves a semi-exposed area and is a great seaweed to cut and gather from a kayak or other craft, as its tresses float on the surface. It is at its best in spring and early summer, before the fronds become somewhat thick and warty.

When it is young and thin it behaves quite similarly to the pasta with which it shares its name, and is equally as delicious in a tomato sauce.

Spaghetti de mer is a prized food in France, where it is often marinated or pickled. It is valued for its nutty taste, rather than tasting especially of the sea.

Sea spaghetti was once burned for kelp on the Aran Islands, but otherwise it has no history as a commercial seaweed. Its Irish name is *rúalach*.

When you cook sea spaghetti, it turns bright green and looks even more appetising, and cooking is recommended as the plant matures. Eaten young, you can enjoy it raw in a salad or pickle.

the seaweeds
atlantic wakame

Atlantic Wakame, or *alaria esculenta* prefers freezing waters on a sheer rocky wall in a wave-smashed exposed coastline, and is only found on extreme lows.

This can make it challenging to harvest, but it is worth the effort for its sweet accessible flavour.

In Ireland Atlantic wakame has attractive common names: tangle, dabberlocks, and honeyware. It is also known as wing kelp, and its Latin name *alaria* also translates as "wings".

Atlantic wakame tastes similar to Japanese wakame, *undaria pinnatifida*, and both are characterised by a prominent central rib. But they belong to two separate species, and whilst *alaria* is fairly scarce, *undaria* is listed as being amongst the top 100 of the world's worst invasive species.

Atlantic wakame is a late-spring, early-summer treat, after which the fronds start to break up and disintegrate in what it considers hostile warmer, calmer seas. The plant grows more happily during winter, but is not ready for harvesting during these colder months. Sustainable harvesting begins in March and strictly the upper third of the frond should be harvested with a knife, leaving the base of the frond, the wings, the stipe and the holdfast.

A small amount of Atlantic wakame is commercially farmed in Ireland, where it is grown on ropes. Like its Japanese equivalent, Atlantic wakame is good for flavouring soups, sauces and salads.

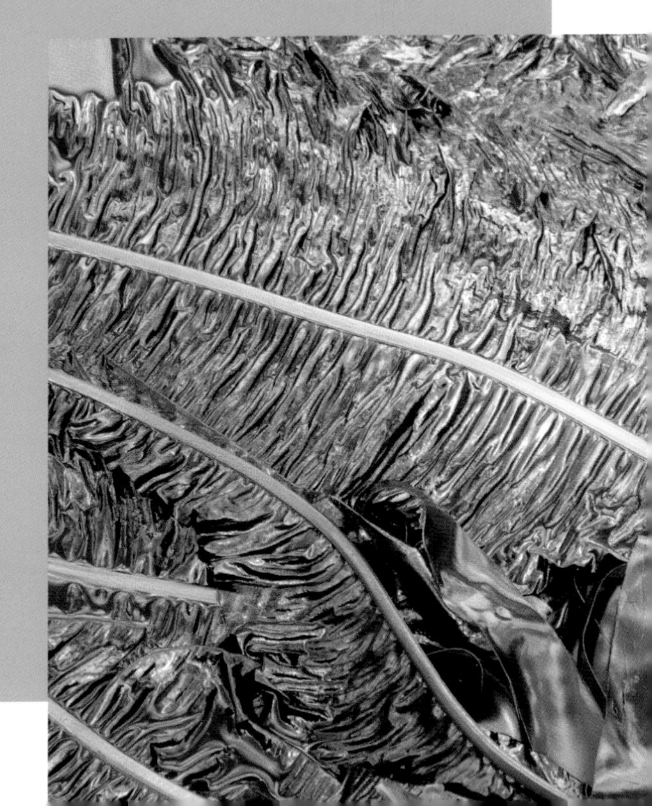

kelp (kombu)

We use the word kelp to describe the thick forests of giant seaweed that reside at the lower reaches of the tide. But it is only relatively recently that this word has been used in a naming context. Originally the word kelp referred to the burnt ash (sodium carbonate) that was made from the brown seaweed harvest.

There are two varieties of kelp that look very similar: one is oarweed, the other forest kelp. To tell them apart you need to look at how they stand at low tide. Forest kelp, *laminaria hyperborea*, has a stiff mucus-producing stipe that was traditionally harvested for alginic acid, and it stands erect in the water, visible at spring lows. Oarweed, *laminaria digitata*, is found between the neap and spring lows, and lies flat when exposed on the shore.

In late spring, the fronds of forest kelp become detached, allowing for new growth from the stipe. The fronds that are cast up on the shore are known as Mayweed, *múrach bealtaine*, while the stipe is still known as sea-rod, or *stúmpa*.

Kelps are also known by the Japanese word for them, *kombu*, and *kombu* is hugely significant in the discovery, by Japanese chemist Kikunae Ikeda, of the so-called fifth taste, *umami* (taken from *umai*, meaning delicious, and *mi*, meaning essence, or taste).

Ikeda discovered this taste in seaweed in 1908, but the taste was only given credence in the west nearly 100 years later when *umami* taste receptors were confirmed scientifically, on both the human tongue and in the stomach.

the seaweeds
sugar kelp

Sugar kelp, known as *kombu royale*, also has the descriptive name of sea belt. The sweetness alluded to in its name comes from *mannitol*, a sweet-tasting sugar alcohol, which has about *60% of the relative sweetness of sucrose. Sugar kelp is rich in *mannitol*.

Mannitol itself gets its name from *manna*, implying that this is food of the gods! You can see the *mannitol* on dried seaweed as a white powder. It is a sign of good ageing, and it should never be washed off.

Sugar kelp – *laminaria saccharina*, or *saccharina latissima* as it is also known – is the closest species to the *saccharina japonica* that is made into the Japanese soup stock, *dashi*, from which the fifth taste, *umami*, was discovered. But the North Atlantic seaweed is also high in viscous alginates, which make it excellent for a seaweed bath, but not so suitable for the thin Japanese soup stock. In a paper published on the web, *Seaweeds for the New Nordic Cuisine*, the authors suggested that dilisk is a better North Atlantic seaweed for making *dashi* than *laminaria saccharina*.

Perhaps the most surprising use of sugar kelp is its ability to foretell the weather. Known as "poor man's weather glass" the seaweed is known to go brittle on the approach of a high pressure system, and limp in advance of a low.

* Seaweeds for umami flavour in the New Nordic Cuisine was published by http//:www.flavourjournal.com/content/1/1/4 in 2012

shore profile

The shore profile of seaweed is a predictable one, with seaweeds thriving in places depending on how tolerant they are of being covered by water, or being exposed to light and air.

Scientific investigation of the seaweed of these islands began in the 18th century and, since then, over 500 different species of seaweed have been identified here. Of these a fraction are harvested commercially, and only a very small number are eaten.

Ireland has over 3,000km of coastline, and the UK has nearly 18,000km with shores that are dotted with rocky bays and inlets where seaweed thrives in both the sheltered and exposed areas. Because of our latitude we enjoy both warm and cold-water species.

From the 500 identified species, I have isolated 15 that are good for eating, or for making cosmetics. These are the seaweeds used in this book.

Almost all of these seaweeds are available to buy from licensed seaweed harvesters many of whom sell their products through the internet, as well as through specialist shops. These harvesters do a wonderful job in drying and packaging our seaweed and making them easily available to us.

But the confident seaweed cook should visit the shore and know the seaweeds. And the good news is, they look just like they do in photos – unlike mushrooms – and the differences between them are marked. They are also abundant.

So, you will always find channelled wrack at the very top of the tide, just above the splash zone, and a few metres down you will always find the kelps, only exposed at Spring lows. In between, the wracks dominate, starting with spiral wrack and going down to serrated wrack, which marks the end of the neap low. Rooted to the lower tidal shore will be the sea spaghetti, its fronds floating on the water surface. And alongside the wracks will be the green seaweeds, and underneath them will be the prized dulse and carrageen.

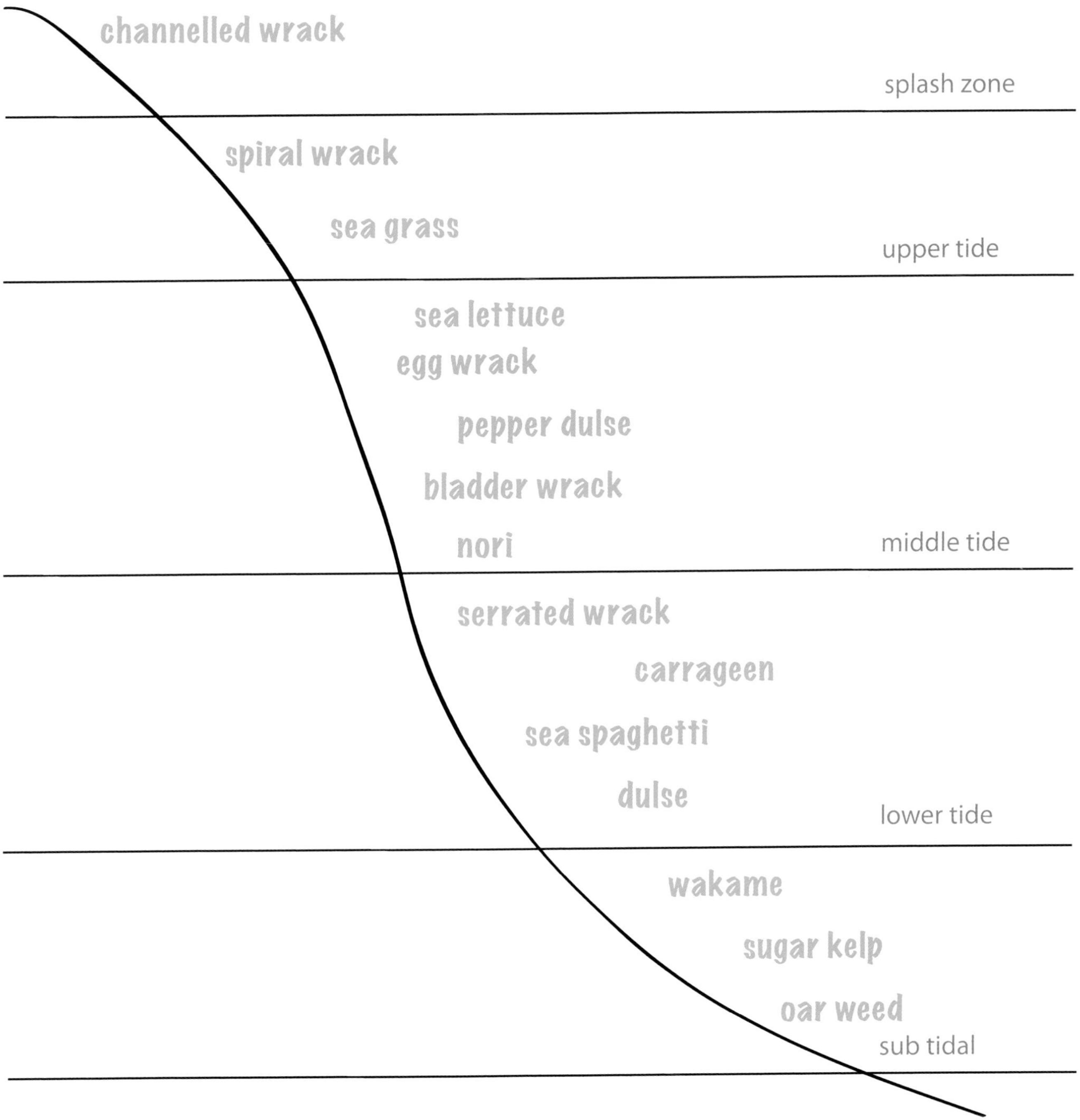

channelled wrack

splash zone

spiral wrack

sea grass

upper tide

sea lettuce

egg wrack

pepper dulse

bladder wrack

nori

middle tide

serrated wrack

carrageen

sea spaghetti

dulse

lower tide

wakame

sugar kelp

oar weed

sub tidal

seaweed size

As a general rule, seaweed gets larger and longer the deeper it grows. This makes perfect sense, when you understand that seaweed is forever reaching for the light. Seaweed contains pigments that absorb light of particular wavelengths. The plants at the top of the tide are often greener and smaller, with pepper dulse the smallest and the brown kelps, at the lower tide, reaching several metres high, and growing quickly.

Here are some of the most common seaweeds positioned beside a Euro coin to show relative sizes.

the relative height of seaweed, compared to a €1 coin >

Pictured opposite, from left to right
Top: pepper dulse, chanelled wrack, carrageen
Middle: dilisk, sea spaghetti, sea lettuce
Bottom: serrated wrack, Atlantic wakame, forest kelp

where to cut

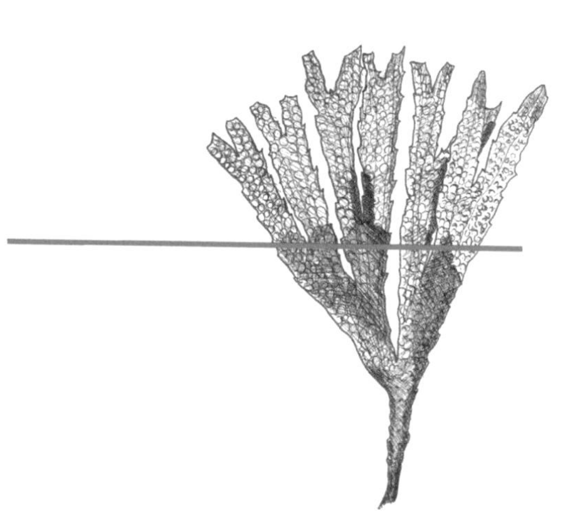

cut wracks well above the stem. Always only take only one or two fronds from each plant.

cut kelps one third of the way up their fronds. Remember, a little goes a long way.

Use a knife, or scissors, when harvesting seaweed.

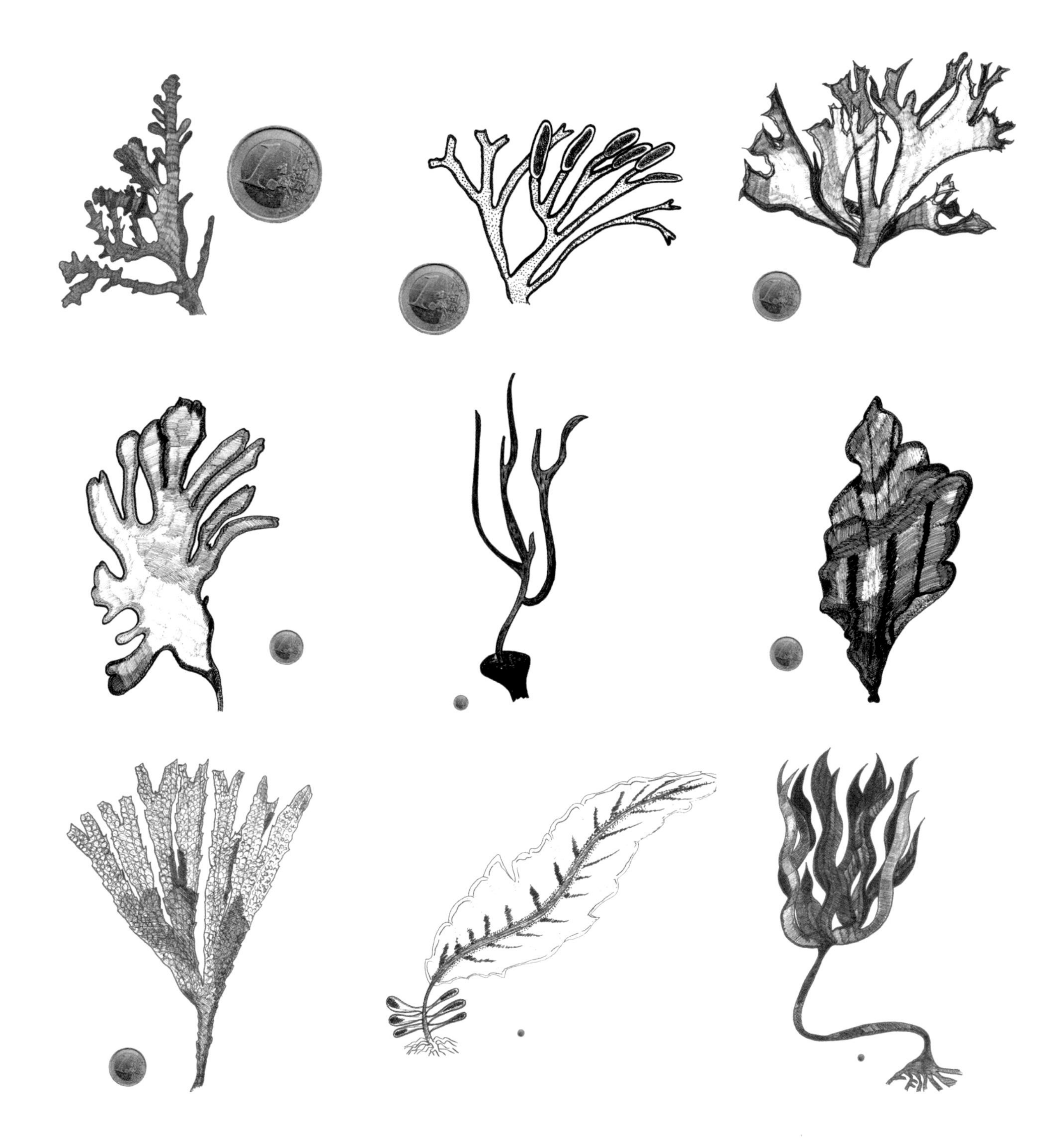

seaweed, equinox & solstice

Head down to the shore one Saturday morning, and you'll find tresses of kelp for the taking in shallow rock pools. Head back at the same time a week later, and it will be as if nothing was ever there. Everything is hidden by a smothering water. For seaweed inhabits an ever-changing marine environment, and the seaweed enthusiast needs to be able to understand and anticipate the tidal cycles.

When the sun and moon align, we get Spring tides.

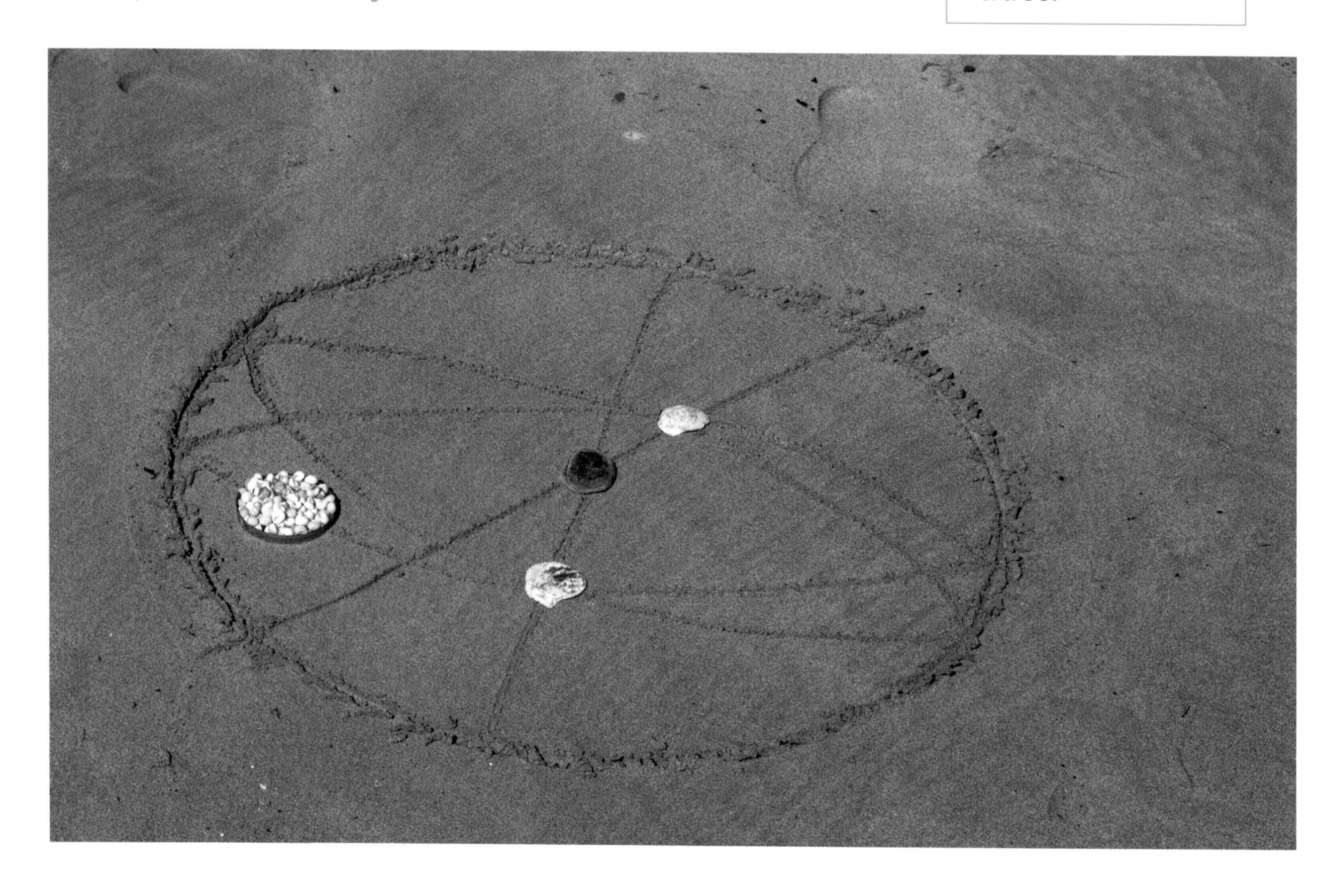

understanding tides

We are part of a grand solar system, which itself is part of an even grander galaxy, which itself is only a minute part of a vast universe. If you were to put a football in a field to represent the sun, then the earth, 25 metres away, would be the size of a peppercorn. If you were then to represent just the very nearest star in our galaxy, *Proxima Centauri*, you'd have to put another, slightly smaller football..... 6,500km away, which from my desk in West Cork, is around about New Delhi.

Years ago, the Ancient Greeks came up with a clever concept that is actually not based on science. The celestial sphere is an imaginary ceiling, a globe, which we see when we look up. We see the Plough, for example, as a selection of stars in that globe, that we have grouped together to form a constellation. There are 88 constellations in our imaginary globe, stars which are actually often very far away from each other and don't physically have any sort of connection. But, using the celestial sphere as an imagined backdrop, we see our sun appearing to move across our sky, always in the same trajectory, travelling from east to west.

In fact, it is not the sun that is moving around us, but we who move around the sun, but we won't worry about that for the moment. The stars behind the ecliptic line that the sun travels in our imaginary celestial sphere, are the constellations of the zodiac.

The other idea to grasp, is that our earth isn't circling the sun from an axis running north-south. If it were, then the sun would stay at the equator. Instead, our earth is tilted 23.5º away from the sun. It is this magical tilt that gives us our seasons. The ecliptic – the line that describes the sun's path in our skies – veers north in the winter, south in the summer. But during the equinoxes – important events for seaweed collectors – the sun is close to zero declination, and has a greater pull on our tide. This is when we get the lowest of the low tides, and is ideal, not only for seaweed collecting, but also for shellfish gathering.

At all other times of the year, we seaweed collectors usually wait for the twice monthly alignment when the sun and the moon are in line.

This is the time of the Spring tide, when the gravitational pull of the moon, and to a lesser extent, the sun, join forces. It happens when we have a new moon and a full moon.

Neap tides, on the other hand, happen when the sun and the moon are not alligned, and pull against each other. During these lesser tides, the kelps remain covered, even at low tide.

If you study seaweed zones, you will find the channelled wrack marks the top of the tide, the serrated wrack marks the neap low, and the forest kelp marks the spring low.

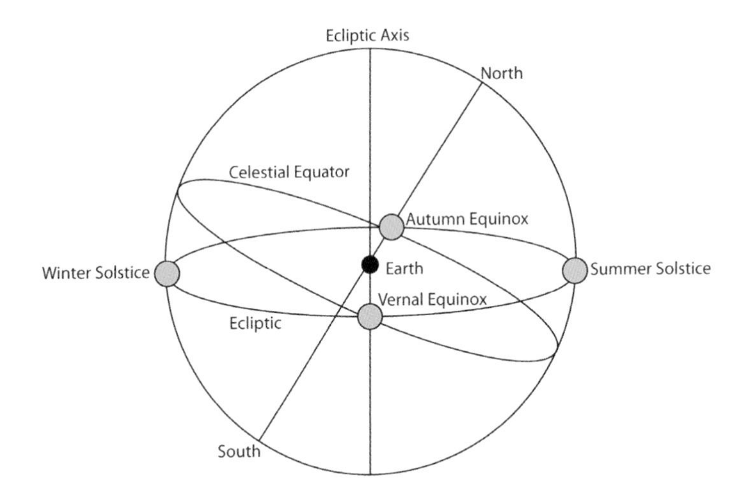

drying & storing

If you visit the shoreline and decide to pick a little seaweed, bear in mind that you will always need less than you think you will. Always harvest using scissors or a knife. You wouldn't pick parsley by the root, and neither should you with seaweed. Take one piece from the top of the leaf of each plant, and try not to disturb either the plant, or the habitat of sea life that resides there.

When you bring it home, it's a good idea to rinse in fresh water. Dry it as you would like to eat it, clean and free of shells, sand and the little sand hoppers that inevitably get caught in its leaves.

After you have rinsed it, a salad spinner does an excellent job in getting rid of excess water.

Thereafter it is easy to dry seaweed. You can hang it on the washing line, leave it out in the sun, put it in a warming cupboard or dry it in a dehydrator.

Whichever method you use, keep returning to the seaweed and tease out the strands, exposing all the surfaces to the air.

In a couple of days (or a couple of hours in a dehydrator) it will be dry, at which point double bag it in sealed ziplock bags.

Technically, if properly dried, seaweed will last for months, but there is no doubt that it deteriorates over time.

Also, seaweed that is ripe and ready to spawn doesn't have the same keeping qualities as young, less oily, seaweed.

I prefer to eat the seaweed I have picked myself fresh, and generally, I only store seaweed that has been professionally harvested and dried.

Red seaweed fossils have been found that date back 1.2 billion years.

understanding seaweed

and now, the science...

"Seaweed tastes like blood!" said the young boy – half repulsed, half in awe at his own bravery in letting these extreme greens get anywhere near his mouth.

We were giving a seaweed talk and tasting at a family day in Cork's Blackrock Observatory. And in this innocent, open observation, he got it so right.

Instead of a vascular system, seaweed is blessed with an abundance of chlorophyll with which it converts light into energy at each point of its makeup.

The young man's observation was so appropriate. He might well have been reading Harold McGee:

"The chlorophyll molecule has a ring structure similar to the heme molecule in animal blood. Instead of iron, it has a magnesium atom at the centre, and it trails a long hydrocarbon tail, called the 'phytyl' group at one end."

McGee continues: *"The phytyl group gives the molecule as a whole the property of being soluble only in fats, and not in water."*

If you put seaweed into very hot water a miracle happens before your eyes. The seaweed goes bright green. This is because the other red and brown coloured pigments dissolve but the green chlorophyll remains, visible in all its glory.

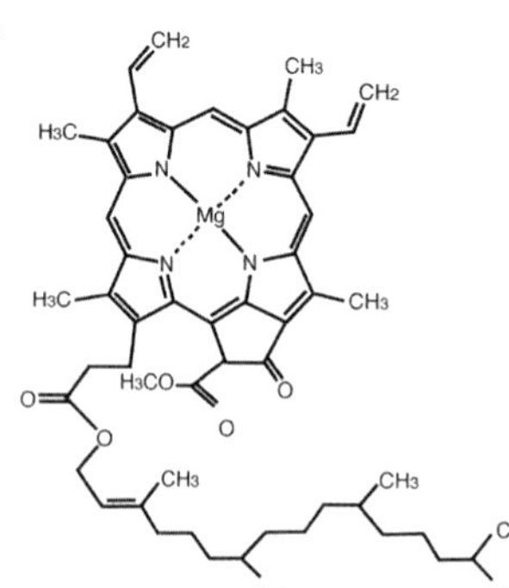

Something similar, though not half so dramatic, happens if you boil broccoli in salted boiling water. It "sets" the colour.

But, if you put seaweed in oil, you get a different effect. This time the oil goes green as the chlorophyll dissolves in it. The oil absorbs all the seaweed health and tastes mildly of the sea.

Top illustration shows an Iron molecule: predominant in blood; lower illustration shows a chlorophyll molecule: predominant in seaweed.

chilli and seaweed oil

Place a fistful of seaweed – serrated wrack or any of the kelps – plus a whole chilli in a Kilner jar. Cover with oil. Use organic sesame oil (not toasted), olive oil, grapeseed or rapeseed oil.

Leave in direct sun, at room temperature for approximately two weeks.

Strain and bottle. You can replace the chilli in the bottles for effect, but this reduces shelf-life.

crispy fried egg

Break an egg into a little jug, or bowl, and – all in one movement – tip into the hot chilli & seaweed oil. After a few moments, gather the white of the egg with a spoon and fold over the yolk. Do this on all sides, until the yolk is covered. Cook for another few moments.

Use the slotted spoon to remove the egg from the frying pan. Serve on toast, dusted with a seaweed sprinkle.

cooking seaweed

seaweed	soup stock drinks sweets	seasoning butter bread	stir-fry salads casseroles	snack sandwich	sushi	pasta noodles	cosmetics
channelled wrack			✓				
spiral & bladder wrack		✓					✓
sea grass		✓		✓	✓		
sea lettuce		✓	✓	✓	✓		
pepper dulse		✓	✓		✓		
nori		✓	✓	✓	✓		
serrated wrack							✓
carrageen	✓						✓
dulse/dilisk	✓	✓	✓	✓	✓	✓	
sea spaghetti			✓	✓	✓	✓	
Atlantic wakame		✓	✓		✓	✓	
kelp	✓	✓	✓				✓

choosing seaweed?

The seaweeds mentioned throughout this book can often be interchanged. In general, the kelps are great for providing a flavour base for stocks or casseroles, and they also have a wonderful viscous nature which makes them good for seaweed baths.

Nori, wakame and dilisk are easy to use, all-rounders that are used in everything from sushi to salads. Carrageen is used for its gelling liquid, great for cosmetics and for drinks as well as mousses. Pepper dulse has a sharp flavour that makes it good for salts and seasonings. The wracks are best dried and milled. Once you get to know the flavours and textures you can mix and match to suit your supply and your own personal taste. See overleaf for more details of individual flavours and textures.

milled seaweed

More and more seaweeds are now available in a milled or ground form. This is a great development for the seaweed cook: ground seaweed is an easy and fantastic addition to almost any recipe. You can, of course, grind the seaweed yourself. If you have a Thermomix, this does a proper job of it, but you can achieve a lot with a good food processor. Coffee grinders and spice mills can have a place too, but seaweed can be tough, and you need something with strong blades. When you have your seaweed milled, which one to use for what is the next question:

Pepper dulse - Reinforces mineral, marine flavours. Good with shellfish and to spice up starchy preparations such as potatoes and pasta.

Sea spaghetti - Has a lovely nutty flavour. Plays a leading role in any casserole or roast.

Kelp (Kombu) - Kelp *enhances* flavour and even our perception of texture. It makes things seem more meaty. This is due to the glutamates pinging our umami receptors. Great to use in the background for soups and casseroles.

Dilisk - Another foreground player for flavour. Use if you want to taste the seaweed. Dilisk pairs well with cheese and other strongly-flavoured foods.

Sea Lettuce and Sea Grass - These two mild-looking leaves actually leave a long aftertaste. Sour sweet. A good seaweed to pair with dairy foods, it cuts richness. This is the strongest milled seaweed for both taste and colour.

Nori - A sweet flavour, and nori flakes delightfully rather than going to a powder. It imparts an Asian flavour and pairs exceptionally well with sesame. Good for sweet dishes also, it goes surprisingly well with chocolate.

Bladderwrack - Bladder wrack gives a real sense of the sea. It tastes and smells like fresh sea water. Great with bread. Makes everything taste like a picnic.

Wakame - Has a sweet pleasant flavour. Traditionally used as a soup garnish, where it expands in liquid to make its presence felt.

seaweed foundations

Seaweed dusts and powders are the great building blocks of Japanese cuisine, most notably the fragrant togarashi and savoury furikake. These seasonings can be used for many different purposes, for coating fish or roast potatoes, or for flavouring rice. They can be used to flavour meats for roasting, or simply to take the place of salt and pepper.

dilisk togarashi

the rind of 1 orange
1 teaspoon black sesame seeds
1 teaspoon white sesame seeds
¼ teaspoon cayenne pepper
1 teaspoon ground ginger
1 teaspoon sichuan peppercorns
1 tablespoon dilisk flakes

Zest the orange, and place the peel on a baking tray. Bake in a moderate 160ºC oven for approximately 40 minutes. Watch! It burns so easily. Cut up into small pieces, and then grind into a powder using a pestle and mortar. Add the rest of the ingredients to the mortar and pound again until you get a powder.

sea lettuce dust

handful dried sea lettuce
1 tablespoon sea salt
1 teaspoon sugar

Grind all the ingredients together into a powder.

chilli dilisk salt

3 tablespoons dried milled dilisk
3 tablespoons chilli flakes
5 tablespoons coarsely ground sea salt

Mix the ingredients together and use to fill a salt or herb mill. (Make sure there are no metal parts, as the salt will cause these to perish.)

Picture right shows (from left to right)
Top row >
1. pepper dulse and fennel seeds
2. milled sea grass or Atlantic spirulina
3. togarashi

Middle row >
1. flaked nori
2. sea lettuce dust
3. milled dilisk

Bottom row >
1. furikake (available in many supermarkets)
2. kuidoraku (available in Asian stores)
3. chilli dilisk sea salt

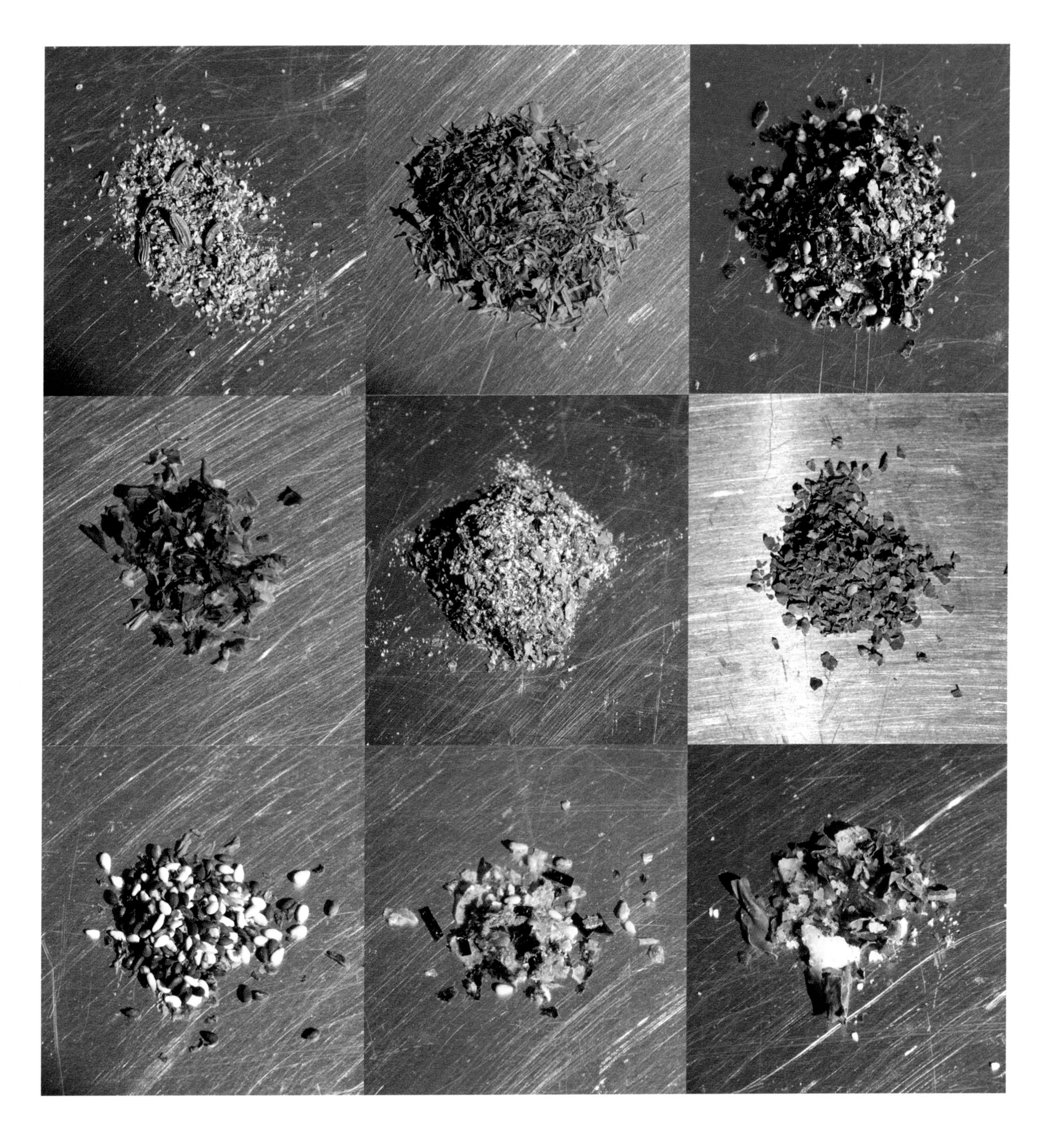

seaweed emulsions

seaweed lemon butter

This is fun if you mix different coloured seaweeds – green gut weed and red dilisk with the yellow coloured lemon rind.

227g butter
handful chopped red and green sea-weed (nori, dilisk, sea grass, sea lettuce)
zest and juice of one lemon
salt

Cream the butter in a mixer, or pound with a pestle and mortar. Add the sea-weed, lemon and season to taste.

nori & wild garlic oil

handful wild garlic leaves
handful dried nori flakes
1 cup good quality olive or rapeseed oil

Roughly chop the garlic leaves and add, with the nori, to a cup of best quality olive or rapeseed oil. Leave to marinate for an hour before using.

Seaweed has twice as much Vitamin C as oranges.

dilisk aioli

1 garlic clove
pinch salt
2 egg yolks
300ml olive oil
juice of 1 lemon
2 tablespoons ground dilisk

Have all the ingredients at room temperature. Pound the garlic and salt, then add to egg yolks. Beat the yolks until thick, then add the oil drip by drip until you get an emulsion. Finally, add the lemon juice and dilisk.

sesame dressing

1 piece sugar kelp
¼ cup organic sesame oil
1 teaspoon mustard powder
1 teaspoon soy sauce
1 teaspoon toasted sesame oil
1 tablespoon black and white sesame seeds

Make a simple dashi by bringing the sugar kelp just up to the boil in some water to cover. Remove a quarter cup of the water (dashi), and then simmer the seaweed for a further five minutes in the remaining liquid. Drain the seaweed and chop finely. Blend the quarter cup of dashi water, oil, mustard, soy sauce and sesame oil. Stir in the sesame seeds and chopped kelp to finish the dressing.

kelp and shiitake rub

1 cup dried shiitake mushrooms
1 stick dried kelp

Snap off the base of the mushrooms, and break the rest into pieces. Break the kelp into pieces too, and place both in a food processor or spice grinder and process/grind until you achieve a smooth grind. Use as a rub for roasting meat, tofu or fish, or to flavour a soup.

nori gomasio

Inspired by Cork's Café Paradiso.

¼ teaspoon salt
5 teaspoons sesame seeds
1 teaspoon nori flakes

Heat a dry frying pan, and toast the salt for a couple of seconds. Place the salt in a mortar. Add the sesame seeds to the hot pan and toast for a few minutes. Do not leave the pan, they burn easily. When seeds turn a caramel and begin to pop, add to the mortar also. Pound the salt, sesame seeds and nori flakes with a pestle, until the seeds break up and you get a rough grain. Use as a seasoning.

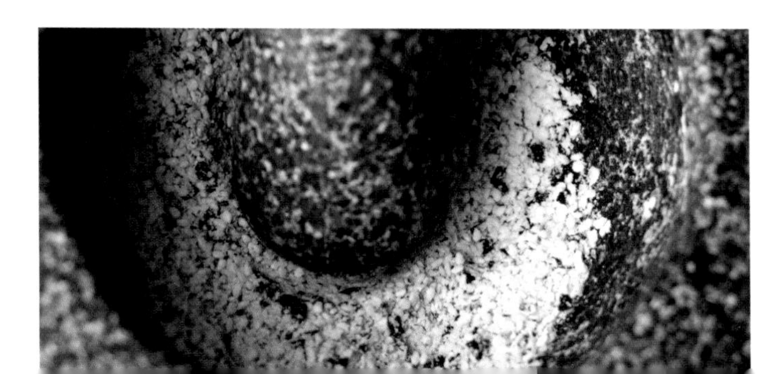

lemon butter sauce with marinated sea spaghetti

The vinegared sea spaghetti makes this simple sauce taste as good as the best restaurant seaweed beurre blanc.

10 fronds sea spaghetti
juice of ½ lemon for marinating
3 tablespoons white wine vinegar
juice of 1 lemon
25g butter
50ml cream

Simmer the sea spaghetti for approximately ten minutes, it will turn a nice shade of green. Drain, chop finely and marinate for an hour in the lemon juice and vinegar.

Mix the juice of 1 lemon, butter and cream together in a small saucepan and heat, beating with a fork to make a liaison sauce. Stir in the marinated sea spaghetti and serve. Good with fish.

sesame & nori vinaigrette

This makes a terrific salad dressing – especially good for grated carrot salad – and a dipping sauce.

¼ cup rice vinegar
1 tablespoons soy sauce
1 teaspoon sugar
⅓ cup dashi
¼ cup sesame seeds
1 teaspoon flaked nori

Mix the vinegar, soy sauce and sugar together over medium heat and stir until the sugar dissolves. Remove from the heat and add the dashi. Toast the sesame seeds in a dry frying pan and then grind to a rough paste, using a pestle and mortar. Stir the sesame seeds and the nori flakes into the cooled vinegar mixture.

sea grass, chilli & fish sauce vinaigrette

Great with grilled meat or vegetables.

¼ cup rice vinegar
1 tablespoon fish sauce
½ red chilli, finely diced
1 teaspoon sugar
1 tablespoon sea grass
juice of 1 lime

Shake all the ingredients together in a jar.

There are over 500 species of seaweed identified around the UK and Irish coastline.

healthy snacks

kale crisps with dilisk

Wash the kale and dry, first in a salad spinner, and then between kitchen paper. The leaves must be totally free of any water. Pull away the stalks, and place on a single layer on an oven tray. Cook one tray at a time. Drizzle over a couple of tablespoons of olive oil per tray, and about a teaspoon of salt. Add some dilisk that you have teased apart into single strands. Stop, to admire the colours, before massaging the oil and salt into the leaves, with your hands, so that everything is coated.

Cook for about 10 minutes in an oven set to 150ºC. Take the kale out when it still has the tiniest modicum of limpness. It will finish crisping on the warm tray. Eat like crisps.

overnight oven-roasted seaweed crisps

Turn the oven up to its highest setting. Place seaweed (kelps or dilisk work best) on a tray. Massage a little cooking oil into the seaweed, so that all surfaces are covered. Place in the oven and turn off the heat. Leave until they crisp. This recipe works well if you place in a hot oven when you finish cooking. By morning they will be crispy.

nettle & sea grass labneh

1 litre natural unsweetened yogurt
bunch of young nettle leaves
handful sea grass

To make yogurt cheese, strain the yogurt in muslin overnight to remove the whey.

Blanch the nettles in salted boiling water for a few seconds to get rid of the sting, then drain, spin in a salad spinner and dry in a dehydrator or a low oven.

Stir the dried nettle leaves and sea grass into the strained yogurt for a lovely zingy soft cheese.

seaweed chilli pop corn

Heat a tablespoon of chilli oil in a large saucepan. Drop 3 or 4 popcorn kernels into the oil and cover the pan. When the kernels pop, add ⅓ cup of popcorn kernels in an even layer. Cover, remove from heat and count 30 seconds. Return the pan to the heat. The popcorn should begin popping. Once the popping starts, gently shake the pan by moving it back and forth over the burner. Keep the lid slightly ajar to let the steam from the popcorn release. Once the popping slows to several seconds between pops, remove the pan from the heat, remove the lid, and shake out the popcorn. Add salt and nori flakes.

bladderwrack bar nuts

Based on a bar nuts recipe from Union Square Café.

150g cashew nuts
2 tablespoons coarsely ground bladderwrack
1 tablespoon chopped rosemary
pinch cayenne & 1 teaspoon sea salt
1 teaspoon brown sugar
15g melted butter

Toast the nuts and bladderwrack in a 190º C oven for about 10 minutes, until they go golden and crispy. Toss with all the other ingredients until the nuts are well coated. Allow to cool.

sandwiches & wraps

There is a long tradition in Ireland of putting seaweed into a sandwich. The classic seaweed sandwich was usually composed of nothing more than white bread, loads of butter and strips of chewy dilisk, a summer treat for teas and picnics.

seaweed pickles

Fifth generation seaweed harvester Ger Talty, of Wild Irish Sea Veg, has a clever demonstration tool when speaking about seaweed at conferences and food events. He mixes sea spaghetti, first in a jar of dill pickles, and then mixes another batch in a can of sweet fruit, such as prunes or peaches in syrup. People taste, and then understand how seaweed takes on the flavours of whatever you combine it with.
And it's also a delicious ingredient for a pickle that goes beautifully in sandwiches.

seaweed Reuben

handful fresh sea spaghetti
1 jar dill pickles
slices of spiced beef
melting cheese, such as Coolea
butter
white pan loaf, sliced

First chop the sea spaghetti. Roughly chop the contents of a jar of dill pickles, as much as you need, and stir in the seaweed. Leave to marinate in the pickle juices for 10 minutes. Sandwich together with the rest of the ingredients, then grill in a panini press or in the oven.

ham sandwich with dilisk crisps

There is no record of the first person to think of putting crisps in a sandwich, but certainly it has become a global practice. But if you're looking for that salty, crispy hit between two slices of bread, a much more healthy alternative is to sprinkle in some crisps made from dilisk (see page 54).

This works brilliantly with the following: butter two slices of brown bread and add a little mayonnaise. On one slice, layer some cooked sliced ham, lettuce leaves, some slices of tomato and cucumber and finally some chopped spring onion. Sprinkle over some toasted dilisk crisps, and top with the other buttered slice. Cut into triangles and serve with more dilisk crisps.

feta dip with nori, dill & mint

200g feta cheese
3 tablespoons olive oil
large handful of fresh mint and
  fresh dill
2 tablespoons nori flakes

Place all the ingredients in a food processor and buzz until the mixture turns to a paste. Serve with good bread.

Salt beef in Ireland was originally not made with salt, but with sea ash, from the remains of burning seaweed.

tuna, egg & sea grass

3 hard boiled eggs, chopped
50g tuna or smoked tuna, flaked
3 tablespoons mayonnaise
1 stick celery, stringed and chopped
1 teaspoon wild garlic capers, or capers
1 tablespoon sea grass
¼ teaspoon mustard

Mix together, and sandwich between white bread with butter and lettuce.

buckwheat & sea lettuce tofu pancake wrap

300g buckwheat flour
salt and pepper
2 tablespoons ground sea lettuce
1 egg
900ml milk

In a large bowl, stir together the flour, salt and pepper and ground sea lettuce. Beat the egg into the milk, then whisk the liquid into the flour. Leave to settle for about 20 minutes and then use to make pancakes. Heat a frying pan, rub oil around the base using a piece of kitchen paper. Spoon a ladleful of pancake mix into the centre of the pan and allow it to seep to the sides. The surface should bubble slightly. Turn over and cook the other side. Fill with marinated tofu (see page 71), sauerkraut and salad for a delicious, healthy wrap.

seaweed basics

dashi & soups

Dashi, which translates into English as 'extraction', was the vehicle with which Japanese chemist Kikunae Ikeda discovered what we now accord to be the fifth taste, *umami*. Dr Ikeda isolated a flavourful molecule in the amino acid *glutamate* and coined the term to describe the fifth taste – the other tastes being salty, sweet, sour and bitter.

Umami was only accepted as a taste in the West 100 years after Ikeda's discovery, when physical taste receptors of *glutamate* were confirmed by science. Interestingly, we have *umami* taste receptors not only on our tongues but also in our stomachs, where they alert our digestive systems. Since its discovery in seaweed, *umami* flavour has been identified in many different foods, including Parmesan, ripe tomatoes, cured anchovies – and mother's milk.

Dashi works, not by being intrinsically strong in flavour, but by enhancing whatever you add to it, improving both its taste and its texture.

Foods with an *umami* background seem to become heartier and fuller, and the flavour-sensation actually helps our stomachs to prepare for proteins and their digestion.

The *umami* flavour, coming from the *glutamates* in seaweed, acts like a highlighter pen on printed type. The yellow highlighter on its own would say very little, but apply it to text, and it glows.

sugar kelp dashi (left), dilisk dashi (right) >

making dashi

Traditionally, this simple soup stock is made with Japanese kombu. The closest North Atlantic seaweed we have to *saccharina japonica* is sugar kelp. Another seaweed with a glutamate punch strong enough to flavour this stock is dilisk. Sugar kelp dashi is darker and fuller. Dilisk makes a dashi that is light and fresh.

Do not rinse the seaweed, and it is important *not to let it boil*. If that happens it makes the stock bitter. So please follow instructions carefully.

1 litre water
20g dilisk or sugar kelp (do not wash)
2 tablespoons dried bonito flakes
a dash of sake
a few drops soy sauce
salt to taste

Put the cold water and seaweed into a saucepan and bring very slowly to the boil. Just as it gets to the boil, remove the seaweed.

Place on the heat again for a second to bring it up to boiling point and then take off the stove altogether. Stir in the bonito flakes, and leave until they begin to sink to the bottom of the liquid.

Strain through muslin, and then season the stock with sake, soy and salt.

overnight no-boil dashi

An alternative recipe for a simple dashi, made with seaweed can be produced by marinating a piece of sugar kelp in some water overnight. (No need to boil.) The following morning remove the seaweed.

shiitake dashi, vegetarian broth

Make a dashi, and then use the liquid to poach six dried shiitake mushrooms for around 30 minutes. Remove the mushrooms, which can be served as an ingredient in the soup or noodles.

soup or noodle broth

Heat together 1 litre dashi, 1 teaspoon salt, ¼ cup soy sauce, 1 tablespooon sugar, 1 tablespoon mirin. Use this liquid to make soup or noodle dishes.

suimono soup

In Japan, suimono soup is traditionally served after the main course, always artistically arranged and usually served in a little lacquered lidded bowl.

Take care in the placing of ingredients. Place 2 to 3 ingredients in the bowl, before pouring over some hot broth, being careful not to damage the design. Ingredients that are suitable for suimono are: poached white fish; prawns or shrimp; quail's eggs; tofu; sliced green beans; omelette; snow peas; miso; sliced pork; spring onions; spinach and seaweed.

seaweed stock paste

The French word for soup base, *fond*, means foundation; the English word, stock, comes from the verb 'to provision'.

This recipe for a home-made stock paste is adapted from the recipe book that is given with a Thermomix. It's a paste that will last for six months in the fridge, and, with the addition of 400ml of water to a heaped tablespoon of paste makes an umami base for soups, stews and gravies.

200g Grana Padano cheese or Parmesan
200g celery
2 large carrots
1 onion
1 tomato
1 courgette
2 cloves garlic, peeled
100g mushrooms
1 bay leaf
handful of parsley, sage and rosemary
30ml white wine
1 tablespoon olive oil
1 tablespoon ground sugar kelp
200g sea salt

Grate the cheese very finely and reserve. Chop all the vegetables and herbs, and buzz in a food processor until chopped quite finely. Put all the vegetables into a saucepan and add the wine, oil, kelp and salt. Simmer over a relatively high heat for about 25 minutes, then blend again in the food processor, along with the cheese, until everything turns into a paste.

Bottle in clean jars. Store in the fridge.

There are over 10,000 species of seaweed worldwide.

mussel, coconut & kelp soup

1kg mussels
1 stick celery
3cm ginger
3cm fresh turmeric
1 clove garlic
1 tablespoon olive oil
knob of butter
1 tablespoon ground kelp (kombu)
200ml coconut milk
splash sherry
1 cup water
salt and freshly ground pepper

Wash the mussels, and discard any that don't close.

Put a large saucepan on the heat and empty the mussels into the hot pan, and close the lid. Leave for approximately 4 minutes by which time all the mussels should have opened. Discard any that don't open.

Strain the mussels into a large jug, retaining all the juices. Shell approximately three quarters of them, leaving some in the shell for presentation.

Chop the celery, and peel and grate both the ginger and the turmeric (you can use 1 tablespoon turmeric powder if you can't get fresh).

Sauté the chopped celery and garlic in the olive oil and butter, with the kelp. When the vegetables are soft add the turmeric, ginger, the coconut milk, the sherry, the juices from the mussels and a cup of water.

Cook the soup for a few minutes, taste for seasoning, and finally add the mussels. Reheat, and garnish with celery leaves.

< oar weed, forest kelp, sugar kelp & Atlantic wakame

potato & onion miso soup

This recipe was inspired by a soup made by a young student at a demo in the Ballymaloe Cookery School - thank you Satoko Shibata for the inspiration.

800ml water
1 piece sugar kelp
450g potatoes, peeled and sliced
75g onion, very finely sliced
salt
4 tablespoons sweet white miso

If you think of it, then the night before you make the soup leave the kelp in the water overnight to make the dashi. Otherwise, place the seaweed in the water and bring very slowly up to a boil, removing the seaweed before the dashi has boiled. This is your dashi stock.

Slice the potatoes into 1cm slices and place in a bowl of water for about 5 or 6 minutes to remove some of the starch.

Drain the potatoes, and add to dashi. Bring to a boil, and then simmer on a gentle heat, until the potato has softened, about 6 minutes. When the potatoes are soft, and begin to break up, add the onion, and cook a further 5 minutes until the onions are cooked. Season with salt, bearing in mind that the miso will season it further.

Put the white miso into a bowl, and gradually add some of the warm soup, stirring with each addition, until the miso is loosened and thin. After adding about 5 tablespoons, then pour the now runny miso back into the hot soup. Be careful not to boil the soup after the miso has been added.

Ladle into small bowls and serve immediately.

Nori is known as the "dandelion of the sea".

smoked haddock chowder

This is from a recipe by Paul Flynn of The Tannery, in County Waterford.

600ml milk and 225ml cream
300ml chicken stock
1 onion, sliced
pinch white pepper
4 bay leaves
350g smoked haddock
25g flour, mixed into a paste with 25g of soft butter
1 teaspoon mustard
2 large potatoes, baked or steamed, then peeled and diced into 1cm cubes
a few sprigs of chervil, chopped

raisin, caper & dilisk butter

125g butter
¼ cup raisins, soaked for a few hours in ½ cup of water
⅓ cup capers
grated zest of 1 lemon
handful of snipped chives
tablespoon finely chopped dilisk

Bring the milk, cream & stock to the boil and add the onion, pepper and bay leaves. Add the haddock and poach for 4-5 minutes. When cooked, drain the milk mixture into another pot and boil to reduce a little. Whisk the flour and butter paste into the milk, bit by bit, until it forms a creamy consistency. Add the mustard, then the flaked haddock and the diced potatoes. Heat for 2-3 minutes, without boiling. Season. Mix the butter ingredients and use to garnish the soup.

sweetcorn and kelp soup

4 potatoes, diced
1 onion, chopped
1 tablespoon ground kelp (kombu)
3 cloves garlic, chopped
2 tablespoons olive oil
300g sweetcorn (frozen)
750ml water, stock or dashi

Soak the potatoes in water for five minutes, while you sauté the onion, kelp and garlic in the oil. Drain potatoes and add to the onion along with the stock and sweetcorn. Cook for 20 minutes until the potatoes are completely soft and cooked right through. Purée to a smooth soup and serve with double cream and cheese & sea grass melted on toast.

noodles & pasta

slow-cooked roast pork

shoulder of pork
salt and black pepper
sugar

Rub the pork with salt and sugar and some black pepper. Roast, uncovered in a 160ºC oven for about 5-6 hours. After about two hours, baste regularly with the pan juices.

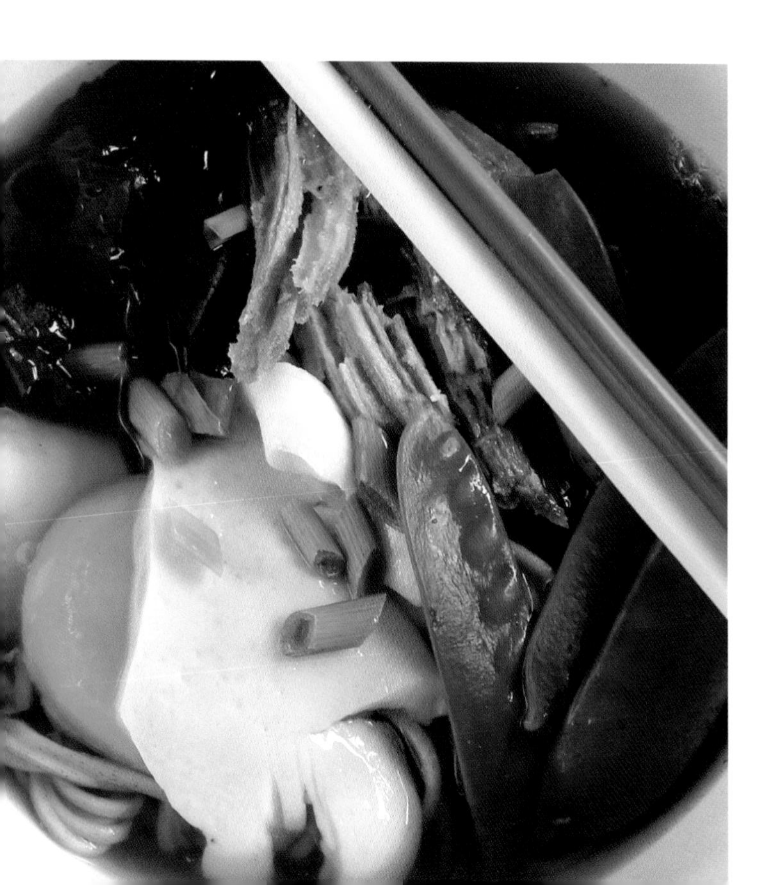

rich soup stock

1 litre dashi
350ml pork stock, roasting juices, gravy or rich chicken stock

ramen noodles

possible garnishes are
shredded slow-cooked pork
marinated, roasted tofu
mange tout
poached eggs
ramen noodles
soup stock
spring onions
seaweed

Bring a pan of water to the boil. Blanch the mange tout. Remove. Poach the eggs. Remove. Finally, cook the noodles.

In another saucepan, heat the stock.

When ready to eat, place some noodles in a bowl and arrange the other ingredients on top. Use an odd number of ingredients, three or five. Ladle over the soup stock. Serve with chopsticks and a spoon.

marinated, roasted tofu

350g firm tofu

1 tablespoon shiitake & sugar kelp rub (see page 52)
1 tablespoon chilli flakes
1 tablespoon sesame seeds
1 tablespoon rice syrup
1 tablespoon soy sauce
1 tablespoon vegetable oil
salt and ground black pepper

Remove tofu from its packet and squeeze out as much water as you can. Wrap in kitchen paper and place between two weighted plates for 15 minutes. Mix together rub, chilli and sesame seeds. Spoon in the syrup and mash with a spoon to make a paste. Loosen the paste with the soy sauce and vegetable oil. Season lightly with salt, and with plenty of pepper. Rub the marinade ingredients into some sliced tofu, and roast in a 180ºC oven for 20 minutes, turning once.

spaghetti and sea spaghetti with a tomato fennel sauce

80g spaghetti, per serving, cooked
20g sea spaghetti, per serving, cut to the same length as the pasta, add to pasta during last 5 mins of cooking.

tomato fennel sauce

1 teaspoon fennel seeds
½ onion
1 clove garlic
olive oil
400g can plum tomatoes

Crush the fennel seeds. Sauté onion, garlic and fennel seeds until onion is soft. Add the tomatoes and cook for 30 minutes. Season with salt and black pepper.

ham, cabbage & dilisk lasagne

½ head green cabbage
100g cooked ham
½ onion
2 cloves garlic
60g butter, plus extra for topping
60g plain flour
600ml milk
nutmeg
1 tablespoon ground dilisk
20g Parmesan plus extra for topping
small handful dried whole pieces of dilisk
250g lasagne

Cut the core from the cabbage and separate the leaves. Steam for 5 minutes. Check that no firm core pieces remain. Slice the ham thinly.

Finely chop the onion and garlic and sauté in the butter until soft. Add the flour to make a roux, and then gradually add the milk, stirring all the time. Bring to the boil and stir until thickened. Simmer for 3 minutes, then season with the ground dilisk, grated Parmesan and a generous grating of fresh nutmeg.

Spoon a quarter of the white sauce into a casserole dish. Divide the ham and cabbage into three portions. Layer one third of the ham, cabbage, lasagne, white sauce, and then repeat the layers, finishing with a layer of white sauce. Grate over some more cheese and butter shavings. Bake in an oven preheated to 190ºC for approximately 40 minutes.

oven-baked seaweed polenta

1 cup polenta
5 cups water
2oz butter
salt
mixed seaweed salad
butter for greasing the casserole
Parmesan

Preheat the oven to 180ºC. Generously rub the inside of an ovenproof casserole with butter. Add the polenta, water, butter and salt and stir with a fork until blended. Sprinkle over the seaweed and place the whole casserole in the oven (you can use an ovenproof frying pan instead). Bake, uncovered, for an hour, or until the polenta is soft and wobbly. Spoon out and serve with grated Parmesan.

Wracks are high in Vitamin A in summer, and high in Vitamin C in the autumn.

albacore tuna carbonara

1 thickly-cut tuna steak, on the bone
juice of half a lemon
1 tablespoon olive oil
1 handful fresh sea grass, finely chopped or milled in food processor
1 clove garlic, finely chopped
1 egg, beaten
50g grated Parmesan
200ml cream
100g butter, soft
sea salt and freshly ground black pepper
200g broccoli
500g penne

Poach the tuna steak gently in a mix of water, lemon juice and olive oil, until it is just cooked, and still moist – it is important that the tuna is not dry, so don't overcook. It should still be pink in the centre. Remove from the poaching liquid and leave to cool. Pull the fish away from the bone and flake roughly.

In a large bowl, toss in the chopped sea grass, chopped garlic, beaten egg, grated Parmesan, cream, soft butter, flaked tuna and a generous sprinkling of sea salt and black pepper.

In a separate pan, cook the broccoli in heavily-salted boiling water.

Cook the penne until al dente.

Drain the hot pasta and add it immediately to the ingredients in the bowl. Toss gently until everything is mixed, and the egg cooks in the ambient heat, then add in the hot cooked broccoli and toss together.

Bring the bowl to the table and serve into warmed dishes, with more Parmesan and some good olive oil.

Seawater contains almost the same concentration of minerals & elements as human plasma, and its sodium content matches that of human blood.

cockles in kelp and tomato sauce

cockles - about 10 per person, or whatever you've managed to find

olive oil
2 cloves garlic
500g fresh ripe tomatoes (or 1 400g can Italian plum tomatoes)
chilli flakes
1 tablespoon ground kelp or kombu
parsley
400g pasta

Parmesan cheese, and tomato sauce, like seaweed, contain the special umami taste.

Place the cockles in a shallow saucepan and put the saucepan on the heat. As they open, carefully remove the cockles and extract their meat, "washing" each mollusc in a little cooking liquid to remove any salt. Discard any that don't open. Strain the cockle liquid through a fine sieve lined with muslin. This should remove the sand and leave you with cockles and cockle juice.

Saute the garlic in the olive oil, and add the tomatoes. Cook until the tomatoes make a sauce, and then add the cockle juice, the chilli, seaweed and the parsley. Add the cockles, and then season to taste.

Meanwhile, cook the pasta and serve with the tomato seafood sauce, garnished with more parsley.

rice & sushi

Mention the word 'seaweed' and most people think of sushi, our favourite Japanese snack. Sushi is generally wrapped in Japanese nori, which is similar to our own species of seaweed, but sushi nori has undergone a toasting process that transforms it from a limp lettuce-like structure to the neat dark green squares that behave in such an accommodating manner, wrapping themselves around the sticky rice.

Making sushi is a fun thing to do at home, as long as you maintain deference to the *shokunin*, the sushi masters who are awesomely skilled in the art. These are the experts who always pick up exactly the same number of grains, whose rice grains all point in the same direction, whose maki fillings are always in the very centre of the sushi. We, on the other hand, simply squeeze rice into tasty wads, and it will always be so, but it's still delicious.

butterflied prawn topping

To prepare raw prawns for nigiri, first snap off the prawn heads, trying at the same time to pull out as much of the vein at the backbone as possible without removing the shell. Using a skewer, spear through the leg side of the prawns, without piercing the flesh. This is to prevent the fish from curling. Pour some salted water into a shallow saucepan – enough to cover the prawns – bring to the boil and then add the prawns and simmer the shellfish for 2 minutes. Remove and plunge into ice water. When cold (about 5 minutes), remove and peel. Make an incision along the leg side of the prawn, open and flatten.

Picture right shows (from left to right)

Top row >
1. inside-out sushi
2. Japanese omelette sushi
3. battleship sushi

Middle row >
1. vegetarian sushi
2. smoked salmon nigiri
3. hosomaki

Bottom row >
1. scattered sushi (all separate)
2. The Californian
3. butterfly prawn nigiri

sushi rice

250g sushi rice
400ml water
1 piece of kelp (kombu)

vinegar mixture
3 tablespoons rice vinegar
1 tablespoon mirin
1 tablespoon sugar
1 tablespoon salt

Put the rice into a pot of water, and swish with your fingers until the water goes cloudy. Pour the water away. Repeat this process about three to four times, then place the rice in a sieve and run water through it until the water is almost clear. Drain the rice for an hour in the sieve.

Place the drained rice and 400ml water and the kelp in a saucepan with tight-fitting lid. Bring to the boil and remove the seaweed. Simmer the rice on a high heat with the lid on. If it threatens to boil over, turn down the heat slightly. Cook for about 5 minutes, until the starchy water no longer rises to the top of the pan. Lower the heat and cook the rice for 15 minutes, making sure never to remove the lid of the pan while the rice cooks.

Wrap the lid in a clean tea towel and re-cover the pan. Remove from the heat, but leave the rice to stand, covered with the tea towel, for a further 15 minutes.

Next, place the cooked rice in a flat-bottomed container. You can buy wooden sushi bowls very cheaply in Asian shops. Wood is the material of choice for rice in Japan because it keeps the rice at the correct temperature.

Spread the rice over the base of the bowl, and begin the process of sprinkling on the vinegar mixture, while fanning with either a Japanese fan, or a folded piece of newspaper. While you sprinkle and fan, run a spatula or rice paddle gently through the rice, turning it, cooling it and coating it, being ever careful not to break it.

When the rice reaches room temperature and has absorbed the vinegar mixture it is ready for making sushi.

Unfortunately the rice doesn't last too long before it begins to dry out, so sushi rice should be made on the day it is eaten.

Kelp is recommended to protect against high blood pressure.

nigiri

Nigiri looks like the simplest sushi to make, but don't be deceived. Many a reputable sushi house would hesitate to make nigiri. Nigiri is all about perfection. The word nigiri describes the hand-rolling action. A skilled *shokunin* will always pick up exactly the same number of grains of rice, and they will all point in the same direction. The topping will be fish at its absolute optimum, and the nigiri will probably only be eaten at lunchtime, just after it has been made.

We can still make great nigiri without these skills, using the wonderful fresh Dublin Bay prawns, and our superb smoked salmon. Measure the ball of rice the first time – you should use 20g. After that judge it, but try to keep the sushi the same size. I hesitate to write "squeeze the sushi together" but effectively that is what we, the untrained, do to make the rice ball. Then, take the piece of fish in your left hand and spread a small amount of wasabi on the fish. Place the rice ball on top, close your hand gently to press the two together, and then invert and serve.

maki rolls

Sushi rolls (maki) are made using a bamboo mat. Place a square of nori sushi seaweed on the mat, shiny side down and cover three quarters of the surface with rice. Start with the side that is closest to you, and leave about 10mm of the seaweed with no rice topping at the end furthest from you. The layer of rice should be about 2cm thick.

Top the rice with your filling ingredients. Pictured on page 77 are Vegetarian Sushi filled with lettuce, julienne of carrot, sliced avocado and spring onion; and California Sushi: sliced avocado, cooked prawn, finely sliced cucumber and a little mayonnaise. You can also make the slender hosomaki, which only contains one ingredient, often cucumber, and uses only half the sheet of seaweed.

Have a bowl of water with a splash of rice vinegar beside you as you work. This is to keep your hands wet, which will prevent the rice from sticking. Squash a few rice grains at the end of the seaweed that has no rice topping. This will seal the sushi together. Wet your hands. Starting from the edge that is closest to you, fold the sushi mat over the ingredients, collecting everything as you go, and slowly roll up the nori in the mat. Join the far edge, fastening with the crushed rice grains. Use the mat to put a final good shape on the sushi, and then slice with a sharp wet knife, keeping the knife clean and damp between cutting.

battleship wrap

Make a golf-ball sized ball of sushi, as if you were making nigiri. Cut a piece of seaweed to fit and gently roll around the rice ball, leaving a little seaweed protruding above the rice in order to hold the roe. Fill the topping with roe - we use the trout caviar made by Goatsbridge Trout in County Kilkenny. A couple of pieces of cucumber will make the mast.

inside-out roll

Place a piece of cling film on the bamboo mat, and then place the sushi nori on top. This time, cover the seaweed entirely with a thin layer of rice. Place another sheet of cling film on the rice and invert the seaweed rice using the cling film to help you. Remove the first sheet of cling film and, this time, place the filling ingredients on top of the nori. Roll up, gently removing the cling film as you go. Dip a portion of the rice into a mixture of toasted dilisk and sesame seeds for an extra element of presentation.

rice balls (Onigiri)

Cook the rice, but this time, shape into larger triangles, once again using wet hands. Take a small square of sushi nori, and wrap the base of the rice ball with the seaweed. Sprinkle with a mixture of toasted dilisk and sesame seeds.

Japanese omelette

⅓ cup dashi
½ teaspoon salt
scant tablespoon mirin
scant tablespoon soy sauce
4 eggs
vegetable oil for cooking

Combine the dashi, salt, mirin and soy sauce and stir to dissolve the salt.

Beat the eggs very loosely, using just a pair of chopsticks. You only want them to hold together, they shouldn't be frothy.

Add the dashi liquid to the eggs. Heat a non-stick pan, and smear a little cooking oil over it, using a piece of kitchen paper. Take a ladleful of the egg mixture and add to the hot pan, tipping the pan to cover the surface. As soon as the underside cooks, before the surface has cooked, roll up the mixture using a spatula and the chopsticks to help you. It's easiest if you roll towards you. Move the roll to the side of the pan nearest you, oil again, and add another ladleful of the egg. Roll up again, this time incorporating the first roll. Repeat the process until the egg is used up and you have a long roll of layered omelette. Remove and slice thinly to make egg sushi.

An alternative egg sushi is to place a slice of sushi nori in between the layers of egg while making the omelette.

pickled ginger

225g fresh ginger
2 tablespoons salt
1 cup rice vinegar
¼ cup water
2 tablespoons sugar

Peel and slice the ginger, paper thin, using a mandolin. Salt the slices, and leave for 24 hours. The next day, mix the marinade ingredients together and add the ginger to the marinade in a Kilner jar. Leave in the fridge for a week. The pickle will last for months, and will turn a delicate pink colour in the process.

prawn and sea vegetable paella

1 large onion, finely chopped
3 gloves garlic, finely chopped
2 large tomatoes, roughly chopped
olive oil
saffron threads
500g paella rice
1 litre fish or chicken stock, heated
1 large red pepper, diced
250g prawns, peeled
2 tablespoons milled kelp (kombu)

In a large paella pan, make a sofrito by frying the onion, garlic, chopped tomato in olive oil until the onions are soft and translucent and the tomato is jammy.

Add a pinch of saffron threads and the paella rice, turning over to coat the rice in the jammy mixture. Add the hot stock and stir to mix everything together.

Over a medium heat, cook the rice but do not stir – you want the bottom of the dish to crisp. Scatter the diced pepper on the surface and allow it to cook as the rice absorbs the stock.

When the rice is almost completely cooked, place the peeled prawns on the surface of the dish, and scatter over the kelp. Cover with a large lid and allow to cook through for 3-4 minutes.

Take the paella pan off the heat and allow to rest for a few minutes before serving straight from the pan.

For a summer treat, cook the paella on a barbecue instead of a hob.

Carrageen is also known as — E407

coast

seafood and shellfish

elderflower-cured mackerel

6 ultra fresh mackerel
4 tablespoons sea salt
2 tablespoons caster sugar
6 sprigs of elderflower in full bloom
liberal tablespoon ground kelp (kombu)

Fillet the mackerel, but leave the skin on. Slice away the fine bones at the belly of the fish, then cut either side of the central pin bones, and remove the central bones in one piece.

Place six fillets of mackerel, skin-side down into a container that will fit all six comfortably, pack with the salt, sugar, elderflowers, pepper and seaweed and top with the remaining six fillets, skin-side up. Place a small chopping board on the fish and weigh down with a bag of flour. Marinate for 2-3 days, turning the fish morning and evening. To serve, remove the herbs, scrape off the seasonings and cut into very thin slices.

dill & mustard sauce

4 tablespoons Dijon mustard
1 teaspoon mustard powder
1 tablespoon caster sugar
2 tablespoons white wine vinegar
6 tablespoons vegetable oil
chopped dill

Mix the first four ingredients together in a bowl, then - using a wire whisk - beat in, little by little, 6 tablespoons vegetable oil until it is the consistency of mayonnaise. Stir in 3-4 tablespoons chopped dill.

Bladderwrack has paired bladders. Egg wrack makes one bladder each year. Serrated wrack has no bladders.

steamed monkfish with furikake and wasabi champ

Furikake is a well-known Japanese seasoning that mixes black and white sesame seeds, nori and shiso leaves. You can find it in most supermarkets. It is pronounced "furry car key".

4 portions monkfish (approx 200g per portion)

8-10 medium-sized potatoes
15g butter
1 tablespoon wasabi powder
1 tablespoon wasabi paste
salt and pepper
spring onions

Furikake, to sprinkle
Olive oil & bitter cress flowers

Boil the potatoes until just cooked, drain, reserving the cooking liquid. Mash the potatoes with the butter, seasoning and wasabi. Beat with a fork, adding as much cooking liquid as you need to make a light purée. Stir in some chopped spring onions.

Portion the monkfish into 2cm slices. Heat a steamer over boiling water, and steam the fish slices for approximately one minute.

Transfer the monkfish to warmed plates and serve immediately, sprinkled liberally with some furikake, along with some good olive oil, the wasabi mash and, shown here, bitter cress flowers.

Seaweed uses air bladders to float and catch the sunlight.

grilled scallops with fresh sea grass

3 scallops per person
olive oil
1 tablespoon sea grass, finely chopped
lemon and olive oil preserve (or lemon juice, olive oil, salt and pepper shaken in a jar to make an emulsion)

Brush the scallops with the olive oil. Place your grill pan on the heat until very hot, and cook the scallops for about 2 minutes a side, until charred. Place on a hot plate and sprinkle with chopped fresh sea grass.

Serve with lemon and olive oil emulsion.

seafood crumble with dilisk

There is no better recipe for seafood crumble than this one, from Martin Shanahan, which we first published in our book *Irish Seafood Cookery.* We've added a touch of dilisk to the seafood mixture.

velouté sauce
1 litre fish stock
225ml cream
30g softened butter
30g flour

seafood mixture
900g fresh white fish that has been skinned, boned and cut into cubes
200g carrot
150g leek
half cup dilisk, roughly chopped

crumble topping
100g butter
2 cloves garlic, minced
150g breadcrumbs
2 tablespoons chopped fresh parsley

Preheat the oven to 180ºC. Make a velouté sauce by bringing the stock and cream to the boil. Mix together the butter and the flour, and beat this roux, small piece by small piece, into the liquid. Stir until the sauce thickens.

Steam the fish until just cooked. Grate the carrot, and finely slice the leek.

Melt the butter with the garlic for the crumble topping, then stir the breadcrumbs and the parsley into the garlic butter.

Assemble the dish in an ovenproof casserole: gently stir the fish, vegetables and dilisk into the sauce and pour into the casserole. Top with the garlic breadcrumbs. Bake for 20 mins until golden.

carpaccio of john dory with nori

I learned this simple method of making fish carpaccio from Carmel Somers, of Good Things Café, in Durrus, West Cork. This dish goes beautifully with an avocado and ruby grapefruit salad, or with guacamole.

1 fillet john dory
olive oil
sea salt and freshly ground pepper
nori flakes
cling film

Spread out a sheet of cling film and brush liberally with olive oil. Season the oil with black pepper and nori. Divide one large fillet of john dory into three pieces. Rub each piece with salt.

One at a time, place a piece of fish onto the cling film. Roll a sheet of seasoned oiled cling film over, and beat until thin, with a rolling pin.

Place the ultra thin fillets of fish on a plate, and serve with a fresh salad.

smoked salmon roulades

We used local Toonsbridge West Cork buffalo ricotta and Burren smoked salmon from County Clare.

½ cup ricotta
1 tablespoon flaked Atlantic wakame
salt and pepper
1 tablespoon olive oil
6 slices smoked salmon

Beat together the ricotta, wakame, salt and pepper and olive oil. Wrap in slices of smoked salmon and serve as a canapé or party snack.

pan-fried hake with dill, dilisk and nasturtium capers

50g butter
1 tablespoon nasturtium capers, chopped
handful fresh dill
half clove garlic, chopped
1 tablespoon ground dilisk

4 hake fillets
flour, seasoned with salt and pepper
oil for cooking the fish

Mash the butter with the chopped capers, the chopped herbs and garlic and the dilisk.

Heat a frying pan, then add the oil. Dip the fish in seasoned flour and pan fry for 4 minutes, before turning over and cooking the other side for about 3 minutes, until cooked. The pan should be hot and sizzling to give a good crust to the fish. Put each fillet on a plate, and serve with a tablespoon of the butter.

skate, pepper dulse & thyme fish cakes

250g skate
325g cooked mashed potato
fresh thyme leaves, finely chopped
pepper dulse powder
salt
coarse polenta
cooking oil

Steam the fish until just cooked, allow to cool, peel off the skin and then flake the flesh from the central bone. Gently mix together with the potato, thyme and dulse. Season with salt. Wet your hands, then form the mixture into fish cakes. Dip the cakes into polenta. Dust off the excess, and place in the fridge to rest.

Cook each fish cake in oil for about 4 minutes per side.

squid stuffed with rice, mint and sea grass, with peas

2 small baby squid
100g rice
olive oil
1 small onion, finely chopped
nori, sea grass, mint leaves
1 cup white wine

I large onion, roughly chopped
200g frozen peas
olive oil and butter

If the fishmonger cleans your squid, ask him for the wings and tentacles, as these will be used in the stuffing with the rice.

Rinse the rice to remove the starch, then cook using your preferred method until it is done. Cool under cold water to arrest the cooking.

Whilst the rice is cooking, chop the onion and sauté in olive oil until golden. When the onion is ready, throw in the chopped-up squid tentacles and wings and turn in the onion mixture to cook. Add in the cooked rice, turning carefully, then add a pinch of nori, a pinch of sea grass and finely chopped mint leaves. Spoon the rice stuffing into your squid pouches, but don't pack it in too densely. Close the squid pouches with a toothpick threaded through the top.

Heat a pan, and sauté the squid in olive oil until the flesh turns opaque. Add the cup of white wine, let it bubble for a few seconds, then cover the pan and turn the heat down. Allow at least 30 minutes for the squid to cook to tenderness.

Whilst the squid is cooking, prepare your peas and onions. Chop the onion roughly, and sauté it gently in a tablespoon of butter mixed with a little oil. Cook it slowly, covered, so that the onion softens but doesn't colour, which should take at least 20 minutes. When it is ready, add in the frozen peas, cover and cook until they are heated through. When the squid is ready, remove from the pan, and slice it into rings. Pour any sauce from the squid into the pea and onion mixture, spoon onto a plate and arrange the slices of stuffed squid on top.

socca pancakes & tapenade

Many seaweed harvesters now provide a mixed pack of "sea salad", containing wakame, dilisk, kelp and nori.

sea salad tapenade

25g sea salad (approximately 1 cup dried)
160g green olives
half clove garlic, minced
1 tablespoon capers
4 anchovy fillets
50ml olive oil
1 tablespoon lemon juice
pinch cayenne pepper

Rehydrate the sea salad by soaking in water until it softens. Place all the other ingredients in a food processer and pulse until you achieve a rough purée. Stir in the sea salad.

socca pancakes

120g gram flour
pinch of salt
200ml water
1 tablespoon extra virgin olive oil
oil for frying

A recipe given to me by Susan Holland.

Combine the flour and salt in a mixing bowl. Measure out the water, and add the oil to the water. Whisk the liquid into the flour to make a smooth batter.

Oil a frying pan and heat to a medium-hot temperature. Pour a spoonful of batter into the pan, and tilt the pan to make sure the base is covered with pancake mix. Cook until it browns, and then turn. The pancake should be thin, light and lacy. Fill with steamed or fried fish and tapenade.

whiting steamed in nori with John's mustard dressing

Wrapping fish in nori seems to intensify the fishiness of the fish in the most delightful and fresh way. Eat everything! Fish, skin and seaweed.

John's mustard dressing

½ teaspoon English mustard powder
1 tablespoon lemon juice
1 tablespoon soy sauce
2 tablespoons olive oil

Mix all the ingredients together vigorously.

1 whiting fillet per serving, seasoned with salt and pepper
a bunch of whole nori (not toasted)

Rehydrate the nori in water for about 5 minutes, until it is soft and comes apart. If you pick it fresh, you can skip this step.

Carefully wrap the fish in layers of nori, removing any small stones or shells that might have collected. Stretch the nori around the fillet, you'll be surprised at how large the pieces are when you start to unravel them.

Place the wrapped fillets in a steamer and steam for approximately 5 minutes over boiling water. Slice and serve drizzled with the dressing.

miso, ginger, nori, mussels

2 cloves garlic
2 spring onions
2 tablespoons nori flakes
3cm knob of fresh ginger, grated
1 tablespoon white miso
2 tablespoons sesame oil
1 litre volume fresh mussels
splash of sherry vinegar or saké

Make a paste by smashing the garlic and onion and nori in a mortar and pestle. Mash in the ginger, and finally the miso.

Heat a lidded frying pan until hot and then add the oil. When the oil is smoking hot add the mussels.

Place the lid on the frying pan and leave for a few minutes for the mussels to open. Remove the lid and splash in the sherry vinegar or saké.

Leave again for a couple of minutes until a liquid sauce forms.

Move the mussels to the side of the pan and add the miso paste. Stir in to make a thicker sauce, and then serve the mussels.

Sea vegetables have an ability to remove pollutants from the body. Alginic acids bind with toxins and eliminate them. This is why seaweed is prescribed post-chemotherapy.

seaweed every day

surf and turf

beef, kelp, star anise and turnip hotpot

1kg beef brisket, cubed
sea salt and ground black pepper
8 spring onions
4 garlic cloves
3cm piece of ginger
2 tablespoons sesame or vegetable oil
2 tablespoons ground kelp (kombu)
3 tablespoons Shaoxing rice wine
3 tablespoons soy sauce
3 tablespoons hoisin sauce
2 tablespoons chilli bean paste
3 star anise
1 litre beef, chicken, vegetable stock or dashi
1 small-medium swede turnip

Sea vegetables are ultra efficient photosynthesisers, and have amongst the highest rates of carbon fixation per unit area of any plants on the planet.

Cube the beef and season with salt and pepper. Cut the spring onions into 2.5cm lengths, chop the garlic and the ginger. Heat the oil in a large casserole and fry the spring onions, garlic and ginger for a minute before adding the beef. Cook until the meat is browned then add all the other ingredients, except the turnip.

Cook for about one and a half hours until the beef is very tender. Add the peeled, chopped turnip and cook for a further 30 minutes, or until the turnip is cooked.

Serve with rice and more spring onions to garnish.

roast chicken with kelp, apricot & herb stuffing

60g apricots
tea
75g butter
1 tablespoon olive oil
1 onion, finely chopped
2 slices pancetta
sprigs of thyme and rosemary
1 tablespoon ground kelp (kombu)
150g breadcrumbs
1 chicken

Preheat the oven to 220ºC. Soak the apricots in the tea for more than half an hour. Melt the butter and the oil and gently fry the onion until softened. Add the pancetta and fry that too.

Chop the herbs and combine in a small bowl with the kelp. Stir this into the buttery onions, along with the finely chopped apricots and the breadcrumbs.

Stuff the cavity of the chicken with the stuffing and seal with cocktail sticks. There is no need to truss, you want a good surface to brown the chicken.

Place some peelings, herb stalks, celery, bay leaves and rosemary branches – whatever you have to hand – on the base of the tray and lay the chicken on top, breast side down.

Place in the oven and cook for 15 minutes at this high heat. Then turn the heat down to 190ºC and cook for a further 15 minutes.

Turn the chicken over and roast with the breast side up for 30 minutes, or until you are satisfied that the chicken is cooked through.

chicken & new potatoes steamed in wrack

This is essentially an indoor version of our seaweed fire, or clam bake. This time, you make the "oven" in your largest casserole dish or steamer. You can also use this technique for small lobster, shellfish, whole fish, or mutton. We serve it here with seaweed beurre blanc.

fresh sea wracks gathered from the shore, rinsed with fresh water to remove shells, sand and crabs
part-boned chicken breasts
new potatoes
sea salt and freshly ground black pepper

Place a steamer or rack in the base of the casserole and add 3-4cm water. Pack the casserole with the rinsed fresh seaweed, and then bury the well-seasoned chicken and potatoes inside. Steam, covered with the lid, for half an hour, or until you are satisfied everything is cooked.

Bladder wrack is rich in iodine calcium, magnesium, potassium, sodium and sulfur. All seaweeds remineralise the body.

sea grass and garlic butter

Sea grass is sometimes sold as Irish spirulina, but to get the vivid green effect for this butter, you really need fresh sea grass. It is unmistakable on the beach – the only other thing this green is sea lettuce, which you could substitute, or indeed use a combination of the two green seaweeds. When you get home, dry the seaweed and then put through a food processor or chop very finely.

100g butter
handful fresh sea grass or sea lettuce, dried and chopped finely
2 cloves garlic, finely chopped

Mix together all the ingredients, either in a food processor, or by pounding together in a pestle and mortar.

Place the butter in the centre of a piece of butter paper, and roll up to form a roll. Chill and slice as needed. This butter is great with grilled steak.

Earth's elements are only created when a star goes supernova.

There are over 70 trace elements in sea salt.

kelp and lovage beefburgers

2 large cloves garlic
salt
sprig of lovage
1 tablespoon ground kelp (kombu)
400g good quality beef mince
pepper

Pound the garlic with some salt in a pestle and mortar. Finely mince the lovage and add to the garlic along with the kelp. Pound together for a second. Add to the mince and mix with your hands to make sure everything is combined. Shape into four patties, pressing the meat together well, and making a hollow in the centre of each burger so that it cooks evenly.

To serve, cook the burger on a grill or barbecue, or fry in a frying pan. Serve with relish, in between bread rolls.

BY RORY CONNER
HANDMADE

lamb & dilisk kofta kebabs

500g minced lamb
1 onion, grated
3 cloves garlic, crushed
1 teaspoon dilisk, finely chopped
1 teaspoon cumin, toasted & ground
1 teaspoon cinnamon
sea salt and black pepper
6 mint leaves, finely chopped
8-10 bamboo skewers, soaked in water

Combine all the ingredients, then pulse in a food processor until you have a very coarse paste.

With wet hands, fashion into cigar shapes around the wooden skewers.

Barbecue on a hot grill for approximately 10 minutes, turning only when the kebabs no longer stick to the hot grill. Serve with yogurt, mixed with lemon juice and olive oil.

lamb meatballs with sea stock

500g minced lamb
1 medium onion, grated
2 cloves garlic, minced
3cm piece ginger, grated
50g breadcrumbs, soaked in milk, and drained
1 egg, beaten
1 tsp natural sea stock (see page 112)
sea salt and black pepper to taste
olive oil for cooking

tomato sauce

1 onion, finely chopped
2 slices pancetta, finely chopped
400g can tomatoes, coarsely chopped
thyme leaves
sea salt, black pepper, sugar

To make the meatballs, combine all the ingredients together in a large bowl. With wet hands, form the mixture into golf ball-sized orbs: you should have approximately 30 in total. Heat a tablespoon of olive oil in a large, heavy frying pan, and cook the meatballs until they are evenly coloured all over.

Our seasons and tides are the result of a collision with a Mars-sized asteroid that hit the earth around 4.5 billion years ago, knocking our planet off centre, and leaving it with a tide-creating moon.

Whilst they are cooking, make the tomato sauce. Fry the onion and pancetta in olive oil until the onion is softened, then tip in the tomatoes and throw in the thyme leaves. Simmer until the sauce comes together, then taste and season with salt and pepper, adding a pinch of sugar if needed. Spoon the tomato sauce over the meatballs, and cook together over a moderate heat for 15 minutes.

rack of lamb with a sea grass crust

2 racks of lamb, French trimmed
sea salt and ground black pepper
2 tablespoons mustard
1 slice of bread, crumbed
½ cup ground sea grass (Atlantic spirulina)
1 sprig fresh rosemary
about 7 chives
small sprig of thyme
3 mint leaves

Season the lamb with salt and pepper, then dry cook on the hob in a very hot pan over a high heat to brown the lamb all over. Remove from the pan, and rub the fat of the lamb with mustard. Mix together the breadcrumbs, finely chopped herbs and seaweed. Coat the lamb with this mixture and then cook in a 190ºC oven for approximately 10 minutes, or until the lamb is cooked to your liking.

leg of lamb with anchovy & nori

1 small leg of lamb
3 generous sprigs of fresh rosemary
50g butter
salt and pepper
2 tablespoons nori flakes
1 carrot, sliced lengthways into four
1 onion, cut in quarters
2 stalks of celery, halved lengthways
2 cloves garlic, peeled and bruised with the handle of a knife
350ml potato water, vegetable or lamb stock, or water

Heat the oven to 230ºC. Chop one of the sprigs of rosemary, and mix with the butter, salt and pepper and nori. Smear over the lamb. Place the carrot, onion, celery, garlic and the remaining rosemary on a shallow baking tray and place the lamb on top.

Roast for 20 minutes in the hot oven, then turn down the temperature to 180ºC and roast for 40-60 minutes more, depending on how well cooked you like your meat.

Remove the meat and keep covered to rest while you make the gravy. Place the roasting tray on the hob and pour in the stock or water. Scrape the pan to get all the caramelised bits at the bottom. Then strain the whole lot into a small saucepan, pressing the vegetables, particularly the carrot and the garlic through the sieve.

Don't be tempted to thicken the gravy: this is a lovely, light, rosemary-scented jus.

confit of duck with kelp

2 duck legs
3 tablespoons coarse ground sea salt
ground pepper
2 bay leaves broken into bits
3 star anise
1 sprig of thyme, leaves shredded
1 tablespoon ground kelp
enough duck fat to cover the two legs whilst cooking (you can buy duck fat separately)

First salt the duck with the salt and spices and seaweed. Leave overnight in the mixture.

The next day, wipe off the salt and lay the two legs, skin side down in a casserole that can go both on the hob and in the oven. Cook the duck for about 15 minutes over a low flame, or until the fat runs and the skin browns slightly. Add enough duck fat to completely cover the meat and place in a low oven (150ºC) for 2 hours, until very tender. Put the duck in a crock or jar, and cover with the fat. Leave in the fridge for a week. You can also use lard, if you don't have enough duck fat.

To serve, bring it to room temperature, scrape off the fat and then fry it in the residue of fat that clings to the skin until hot and crispy.

seaweed sausage rolls

The sausagemeat in these sausage rolls has an extra flavouring of Natural Sea Stock* folded into the sausagemeat. This stock is a mixture of ground sea spaghetti, wakame and kelp. Use a good quality sausage meat, and a good quality puff pastry, a generous handful of ground seaweed, and you'll never eat sausage rolls any other way again.

* Natural Sea Stock is one of the seaweed products sold under the Quality Sea Veg label from County Donegal. You could substitute any kombu mix to give an umami flavour to sausage rolls.

buttermilk fried chicken with natural sea stock mix

1 chicken, portioned into 8 pieces, or 6-8 pieces of part-boned chicken breast, chicken legs and thighs.
1 onion
450ml buttermilk
1 teaspoon salt
1 cup flour
1 teaspoon freshly ground black pepper
1 tablespoon natural sea stock
2 cups vegetable oil

Finely grate the onion into a large bowl. Add the buttermilk and a pinch of salt. Add the chicken pieces and marinate for 6-8 hours.

When ready to cook the chicken, remove from the marinade and pat dry.

Put the flour and seasonings into a zip-lock bag. Add the pieces of chicken to the bag one at a time, shaking to make sure they are well coated. Shake off any excess flour.

Heat the oil in a heavy cast-iron frying pan. Heat until the oil ripples on the surface, letting you know that it is hot.

Seaweed contains major fatty acids, including linolenic acid and essential amino acids.

Add the chicken pieces, but don't overcrowd: you will need to fry two batches. Adjust the heat so that the oil is bubbling gently around the chicken pieces. Cover with a lid. Check after 5 minutes, uncover, then cook for another 5 minutes. Turn and cook for 3-5 minutes, covered, and then a further 3-5 minutes, uncovered.

When you are satisfied the chicken is completely cooked through, remove and drain on kitchen paper. Let rest for 10 minutes before serving.

beef stir fry with wakame

400g lean beef

marinade
¼ teaspoon salt
1 teaspoon sugar
1 teaspoon soy sauce
1 tablespoon water
1 teaspoon Shaoxing wine

sauce
1 teaspoon cornflour
5 tablespoons stock
2 tablespoons oyster sauce
1 tablespoon soy sauce

1 piece of Atlantic wakame (de-ribbed)
3 cm knob of ginger
2 cloves garlic
5 spring onions
3 tablespoons vegetable or nut oil
handful of mange tout
handful of baby corn
1 tablespoon tomato purée or cooked tomato
coriander

Chinese noodles to serve

Cut the beef into fine strips. Marinate in the marinade ingredients for approximately half an hour.

If dried, soak the wakame in water for 10 minutes, and then cut into strips.

Chop the ginger and garlic, and slice the spring onions into 2cm pieces.
Put a wok on a high heat until the smoke begins to rise from it. Add the oil and stir-fry, first the ginger, spring onion and garlic briefly, and then with the heat still on high, add the beef in its marinade. Stir-fry for about 5 minutes, by which time the beef will have released quite a lot of liquid. Drain this off into the sauce ingredients, add the corn and mange tout, and a little more oil if you think it necessary then continue to stir-fry for a few minutes longer, until the vegetables are cooked.

Add the squeezed dry wakame and the sauce ingredients. Cook a little longer, adding a little cooked tomato or tomato purée if you think the dish needs a bit of colour.

Garnish with a little chopped coriander and serve with hot Chinese noodles.

Seaweed helps you lose weight by inhibiting the action of an enzyme that controls the digestion of fat. Seaweed fibre also blocks the absorption of fat by the body.

vegetarian

chick pea fritters

250g chick peas, soaked overnight
1 onion
3 cloves garlic
⅓ cup finely chopped parsley
1 tablespoon ground cumin
1 tablespoon ground coriander
1 tablespoon Atlantic wakame flakes
1 teaspoon baking powder
6 tablespoons water
1 teaspoon salt
black pepper
1 teaspoon curry powder
oil for deep frying

Do not cook the chickpeas (it makes the fritters lighter). Drain and place in a food processor. Process until you have ground the chickpeas very finely. Finely chop the onion, and mince the garlic. Mix all the ingredients together and leave to rest for half an hour.

When ready to cook, take lumps of the mixture, about the size of a golf ball. Roll up and flatten slightly, and let rest for a further 15 minutes on a plate. Heat the oil in the deep-fat fryer to 170º, and deep-fry the fritters for about 3-4 minutes until golden brown.

spicy potato wedges

potatoes
vegetable oil
ground dilisk or togarashi powder
1 teaspoon chilli flakes
salt and pepper

Pre-heat the oven to 180ºC. Peel the potatoes and cut into quarters to make wedges. Put some oil in a bowl and add salt, seaweed powder and chilli flakes. Toss the potatoes in the oil, making sure they are covered on all surfaces.

Place the potatoes on a baking tray and put the tray in the oven. Cook for approximately 20 minutes, turning after about 15 minutes when the potatoes no longer stick to the tray. Serve, seasoned with salt and pepper.

warm salad of channelled wrack, carrot and orange

a handful of channelled wrack
3 medium-sized carrots, peeled and cut into batons
50ml soy sauce
splash of apple syrup or apple concentrate
25ml rice vinegar
1 tablespoon finely sliced orange rind
the juice of one orange
60g flaked almonds
cooking oil
large handful flat leaf parsley

For those who follow a vegetarian diet: seaweed is rich in Vitamin B12.

Reconstitute the channelled wrack if dried, by leaving in cold water for about 10 minutes. Place in a saucepan and cover with fresh water. Simmer for about 15 minutes. Remove the seaweed, but reserve the water. Roughly chop the seaweed, removing any stalky bits.

Place the chopped wrack in a wide saucepan and pour over 1 cup of the cooking water. Add the carrots, turn up the heat and cook until the water has reduced to just coat the vegetables. When the water has reduced, add the soy sauce, apple syrup, rice vinegar and orange juice and rind.

Sauté the almonds in the cooking oil, until they go light golden. Watch them carefully, they will burn easily. Add the toasted almonds and the parsley, and serve. Note: this recipe works as a warm salad in itself, but is also good with breast of duck, or pan-fried monkfish.

chickpea, mushroom & dilisk burger

1 tablespoon olive oil (plus extra for brushing the burgers)
2 onions, chopped
150g mushrooms, coarsely chopped
salt
35g Parmesan cheese, grated
60g cheddar, grated
150g can chickpeas, drained
handful dried dilisk finely chopped
100g fresh breadcrumbs
1 tablespoon soy sauce
1 tablespoon wasabi
1 egg, beaten

8 soft bread rolls

To serve:
Green salad leaves, tossed in vinaigrette
slices of tomato, red onion
slices or julienne of radish
mayonnaise

Heat the oil in a frying pan, and fry the chopped onions and mushrooms, seasoned with a bit of salt. When softened, cool slightly and place in a food processor with the rest of the burger ingredients.

Pulse for a minute or so, until the mixture comes together, but be careful not to over mix, or it will get mushy.

With wet hands form into eight burgers and leave for an hour in the fridge to firm up. At this stage the burgers can actually be frozen, and later cooked from frozen.

When ready to eat, brush each burger with some oil and place on a baking try. Bake in an oven preheated to 190ºC for about 15 minutes.

Serve in the bread rolls, garnished with the leaves and salad ingredients. Lastly add some mayonnaise.

young sea spaghetti and pepper dulse >

marinated sea spaghetti salad

This recipe was given to me by Mamiko Crowley, when we did a seaweed demo for the Skibbereen Food Festival.

sea spaghetti

dressing:
2 tablespoons soy sauce
1 tablespoon mirin
1 ½ tablespoons sugar
3 tablespoons malt or rice vinegar
1 teaspoon lemon juice
½ tablespoon sesame oil
chilli flakes

Seaweed depends on sunlight to create energy through photosynthesis.

Cook the spaghetti in boiling water for 5 minutes, then marinate in the dressing for an hour before serving.

channelled wrack and ginger miso slaw

1 head red cabbage, shredded
2 carrots, peeled and cut into thin strips
¼ red onion, peeled and grated
salt and pepper
handful channelled wrack
tablespoon sesame seeds

dressing:
¼ cup white miso
3 tablespoons rice syrup (or other natural sweetener)
¼ cup mirin
3 tablespoons sesame oil
juice of half a lemon
knob of grated ginger

Mix together the cabbage, carrot and onion in a large bowl. Season. Toss well to evenly distribute the onion.

Blend the dressing ingredients together until smooth. Season the dressing to taste with salt and pepper.

Put a saucepan of water on to boil and simmer the channelled wrack for approximately five minutes. Chop the seaweed into bite-size lengths.

Toss the cabbage mixture in approximately half of the dressing (save the remainder in the fridge for another salad).

Stir in the seaweed, and scatter over the sesame seeds.

new potatoes cooked in seawater

1 bucket of clean sea water
new potatoes
butter

Seawater has exactly the same sodium content as human blood. It's a great medium for cooking potatoes or shellfish. The first new potatoes, simmered in seawater from the first days of summer on the beach provoke the Irish phrase: *Go mbeirimíd beo ar an am seo arís:* May we live to see this time again next year.

cucumber & wakame salad

Thanks to Mamiko Crowley for this authentic salad recipe.

½ cucumber, cut in slices and then halved into semi circles
salt
handful of Atlantic wakame
dressing:
1 tablespoon soy sauce
1 tablespoon rice or malt vinegar
1 teaspoon toasted sesame oil

Slice the cucumber and place in a bowl with salt for about 10 minutes. When ready to use, squeeze the cucumber with your fingers to remove the juice. This gives the cucumber a crispy texture.

Reconstitute the wakame in some water for about 10 minutes, and then squeeze out the water.

Mix together the dressing ingredients and toss everything together.

sea spaghetti picnic tortilla

4 eggs, beaten
generous handful sea spaghetti
½ onion, olive oil
3 medium potatoes, peeled

Cook the sea spaghetti for 5-10 minutes in boiling water. Remove, chop, and add to the eggs. Dice the onion and fry in plenty of olive oil until soft.

Dice the potato and add to the onion. Cook until the potato softens. When the potato is cooked, remove and stir into the beaten eggs. Have the oil in the pan very hot, add the egg mixture and cook until the bottom layer is set, and then either place in a hot oven to set the top, or flip over and cook for a minute more.

marinated sea spaghetti

Use this as a base for roasted vegetables and salads of all descriptions.

1 cup dried sea spaghetti
juice of 1 lemon
¼ cup cider vinegar

Cook the sea spaghetti for about 8 minutes, 4 minutes if it's fresh. Drain and marinate in the lemon and vinegar for one hour before using. You can also use the marinade as the base of a dressing, sauce or vinaigrette.

Japanese "as you like" pancakes

Okonomiyaki pancakes are useful for using up leftovers in the kitchen. This recipe is a staple of the Japanese kitchen, and can contain just about any type of vegetable or meat.

5 tablespoons flour
1 teaspoon baking powder
70ml dashi (or water)
2 eggs
½ Dutch or red cabbage
2 carrots
3 spring onions
handful chopped Atlantic wakame
oil for frying the pancakes

Seaweed is ten times higher in calcium than cow's milk.

Okonomiyaki Sauce
¼ cup ketchup
1 tablespoon Worcester sauce
¼ teaspoon dry mustard
1 tablespoon sake
1 teaspoon soy sauce
1 tablespoon honey
pinch ground ginger

Mix together the flour and baking powder, and form a batter with the dashi or water. Beat the two eggs with a fork and add to the flour batter.

Grate the cabbage and carrots, and sliver the spring onions into strips. Rehydrate the wakame in water for 10 minutes if it's dried, and then add to the batter along with the other vegetables. Prepare the Okonomiyaki sauce by combining all the sauce ingredients.

You can make one large pancake, or several small ones. Heat the oil in a saucepan and fry spoonfuls of the pancake until crisp and just cooked.

sea spaghetti & sweetcorn bechamel

25g butter
25g plain flour
300ml milk
sea salt and freshly ground black pepper
nutmeg
1 cup dried sea spaghetti
1 large can sweet corn
Pecorino, Parmesan or Cheddar cheese
butter

Make a bechamel sauce with the butter, flour and milk. Season with salt, pepper and nutmeg. Simmer the sea spaghetti in water for about 8 minutes, then drain. Mix the corn and seaweed in an oven-proof dish, and pour over the bechamel. Top with grated cheese and butter shavings and bake in a 180ºC oven for 20 minutes.

Kombu is a natural food tenderiser: add it when cooking beans and it both speeds up the cooking process and makes the beans more digestible.

kelp condiment

This is a good way of eating up the kelp that has been used to make dashi.

150ml dashi
4 tablespoons soy sauce
2 tablespoons saké
3 tablespoons caster sugar
1 piece of kelp

Place the dashi, soy sauce, saké and sugar into a small saucepan and simmer until it reduces and thickens. Slice the kelp into matchstick slivers and add to the sauce. Simmer for a few minutes before serving.

seaweed & sesame salad with ginger dressing

30g dry mixed seaweed (seaweed salad)
1 teaspoon grated fresh ginger
1 tablespoon rice vinegar
1 tablespoon toasted sesame oil
1 tablespoon soy sauce
1 tablespoon sugar
½ teaspoon salt (to taste)
1 tablespoon sesame seeds
1 spring onion, finely chopped

Put the seaweed in a bowl and cover with water. Leave for 5 minutes to rehydrate. Dry in a salad spinner, or squeeze dry between your fingers.

Grate a small amount of ginger into the bottom of a salad bowl and mix together with the vinegar, sesame oil, soy sauce, sugar and salt.

Toast the sesame seeds briefly in a dry pan, and then add along with the finely chopped spring onion. Toss the seaweed together in the salad dressing.

marrowfat peas with seaweed and mint

500g pack dried marrowfat peas
1 small clove garlic
1 tablespoon wakame
handful fresh mint, chopped
3 tablespoons olive oil
sea salt and freshly ground black pepper
1 spring onion, finely sliced

Soak the peas with the tablet that comes in the box in a pan of boiling water, as per the instructions on the packet.

Rinse the peas carefully, and barely cover with fresh water. Bring to the boil and simmer until the peas soften. Remove any pea skins that rise to the surface. When soft, mash the peas with a fork and fold in the remaining ingredients.

quick pickled white turnip

6 small white turnips with their tops
sea salt
small piece kelp
square lemon rind

Separate the turnip tops from the turnips and wash. Peel the turnips, then grate them into a fine julienne, using a mandoline or a box grater. Peel the leaves from the stalks and chop them finely. Place the julienned turnip and the shredded leaves into a large bowl and sprinkle with a teaspoon of salt. Start to knead the turnips with your hands, turning them over and over and squeezing the vegetable. After a minute, water will begin to be extruded. Keep turning and squeezing with your hands as the water comes out. Discard the water, then place the turnip in a small bowl with the kelp and the lemon rind, and leave for an hour, covered. When ready to serve, lift the pickled turnip from the bowl with a fork and place on a serving dish.

avocado, ruby grapefruit, shaved fennel and toasted Atlantic wakame salad

1 sheet of Atlantic wakame
olive oil
1 ruby grapefruit
1 avocado
half fennel bulb
sea salt and freshly ground pepper

Brush the wakame with olive oil and toast in a 160ºC oven for about 20 mins. Cut the grapefruit into segments and squeeze as much juice as you can from the core.

Slice the avocado and toss the grapefruit slices and the grapefruit juice into the bowl. Shave the fennel as thin as you can and toss with the avocado and grapefruit. Drizzle over olive oil and sprinkle with toasted wakame. Season to taste.

laverbread

You counldn't write a book about seaweed without mentioning sushi, and neither could you get away without printing a recipe for the other famous nori recipe, laverbread.

For what it's worth, this is the most famous recipe to come out of Wales. Seaweed, boiled for hours and then fried, usually with bacon. OK, it's rather more unpreposessing than sushi, and a fair bit of work, but the recipe has endured for a reason, the subtle mixture of tastes between the nori and the oats is a winning flavour.

1 litre volume nori (about 250g)
about 6 tablespoons oatmeal
1 onion, chopped
sea salt and freshly ground black pepper
generous grind of fresh nutmeg
oil and butter or fatty bacon in which to fry the cakes

Forager Mark Williams from Galloway Wild foods writes that in the early part of the season, when the nori is black – around March – four hours boiling is enough to soften the seaweed, increasing to around seven hours in the summertime. You should probably allow a day to prepare the seaweed. First wash it in several changes of water and remove any shells, grit or sandhoppers. Place in a saucepan and add about 200ml water. Bring to a simmer and simmer for several hours, checking the pan regularly and adding more water, a bit like making a risotto. When the seaweed visibly softens and turns glutinous, then blitz in a food processor. Fry the chopped onion until soft, and then beat in, along with the oatmeal and seasonings. Some recipes call for adding bacon to the mix as well if you really want to ramp up the umami flavour.

Take spoonfuls of the mix and fry in ample butter and a little oil. Traditionally served with bacon, laverbread also goes surprisingly well with lamb.

dilisk kimchi

1 head cabbage, shredded
½ cup runner beans, very finely sliced
2 tablespoons salt
4cm piece ginger
8 cloves peeled garlic
¾ cup syrup made from water & 2 tablespoons sugar
handful chopped dilisk
¼ cup soy sauce
¼ cup rice or white malt vinegar
1 carrot, finely julienned
3 spring onions, cut into 2.5cm pieces and halved lengthways.

Carrageen was traditionally fed to horses before market to make their coats more glossy.

Shred the cabbage, and place in a bowl overnight with the runner beans and the salt. The next morning, drain off the liquid and place the cabbage back in the bowl.

Grate the piece of ginger and chop the garlic. Stir both into the syrup, then pour over the cabbage. Add the rest of the ingredients and stir everything together, using your hands.

Transfer to an airtight container, such as a large Kilner jar and store in the fridge for a week.

The kimchi is actually delicious straight away, but then ferments away and can be kept for weeks. Even the liquid can be used – it makes a delicious sauce for noodles.

dilisk, leek and cheddar tart

pastry

160g plain flour
1 teaspoon salt
60g butter
2 tablespoons plus 1 teaspoon cold water

custard filling

3 medium-sized leeks, finely sliced
50g butter
salt and black pepper
handful chopped dilisk
2 eggs
250ml cream
1 tablespoon mustard
100g grated cheese

Put the flour and salt into a bowl. Cut the cold butter up into cubes, and rub into the flour with your fingers. Add the cold water drop by drop, just until the mixture comes together in a ball. Cover with butter paper and refrigerate for an hour until chilled, then roll out and line a 20cm flan dish.

Place the butter paper on top of the pastry, and freeze in the freezer for another couple of hours until hard and frozen. If you want to keep for a longer time in the freezer, then wrap first to protect it.

When you are ready to make the tart, prick the base with a fork, and pre-bake the pastry in an oven preheated to 200ºC for about 10 minutes. There is no need to use baking beans if you are using this pre-frozen dough.

To make the filling: carefully wash the leeks and then sauté in the butter for approximately 5 minutes, until the leeks start to soften. Add about a quarter cup of water, and season with salt. Cover and cook for a further 5 minutes. Season again, this time with black pepper and a good handful of roughly chopped dilisk. Allow to cool slightly.

Beat the eggs in a bowl and stir in the cream, mustard and grated cheese, and finally fold in the cooled leeks.

Pour this custard into the part-cooked pastry shell and bake for approximately 20 minutes, or until the pie is just firm.

This recipe is inspired and informed by the great, influential tart recipes in various books by Deborah Madison.

bread & crackers

malted bladderwrack loaf

2 tablespoons sesame seeds
1 teaspoon coriander seeds
1 tablespoon sunflower seeds
1 tablespoon bladderwrack
1 tablespoon soy sauce

500g malted wholewheat flour
12g dried yeast
1 teaspoon salt
350ml water
Extra sesame seeds for sprinkling

Put a dry frying pan on the heat, and toast the sesame, coriander and sunflower seeds. Add the bladderwrack, and finally splash in some soy sauce. The soy sauce will cling to the seeds.

Combine the flour, yeast and salt and mix in the water to form a dough. Bring the dough ingredients together and then knead for approximately 10 minutes by hand, or a few seconds in a food processor, or using the dough selection of a bread-making machine. Just before the end of kneading, knead in the seed mixture. Allow to rise for about two hours, then punch down and shape into a loaf.

Let rise another hour or so, or until the dough has doubled. Sprinkle with some more sesame seeds, then place on an oven tray and roast in a hot oven, preheated to 200ºC, for 30 to 40 minutes, or until the bread is crusty, and sounds hollow when tapped.

Set on a wire rack and cool before slicing.

This recipe was inspired by a recipe from Patrick Ryan of The Firehouse Bakery.

dilisk & stout brown soda bread

500g wholewheat flour
3 tablespoons milled dilisk
1 teaspoon salt
1 level teaspoon baking soda
1 tablespoon malt syrup
500ml stout (or stout and milk mixed)
5 teaspoons red wine vinegar
1 lb loaf tin, greased

> ***Eating seaweed curbs your appetite and makes you feel full.***

Preheat the oven to 200ºC. Mix together the flour, dilisk, salt and baking soda.

Make a well in the centre of the flour and add the beer, milk (if using), syrup and vinegar. Stir to mix, bringing the mixture together to form a porridge consistency.

Scrape the dough into the loaf tin. It should nearly reach the top.

Bake in the oven for approximately 35 minutes, or until the tip of a knife, inserted into the bread, comes out clean.

Cool on a wire rack before slicing.

kelp and sour cherry scones

250g self-raising flour
½ teaspoon freshly grated nutmeg
1 tablespoon milled kelp (kombu)
pinch of salt
45g sugar
20g butter
100g dried sour morello cherries
150ml buttermilk
sugar for sprinkling
handful flaked almonds

Preheat the oven to 190ºC. Measure out the flour in a large bowl. Grate in the nutmeg, kelp and salt. Add the sugar and then rub in the butter. Add the cherries and finally the buttermilk, kneading very lightly, just until the mixture comes together to form a dough.

Place on a floured board and cut out circles or squares – the dough should be quite thick; scones don't rise that much.

Sprinkle liberally with sugar and press in some flaked almonds. Bake on a greased tray in the oven for 15 minutes, or until cooked and golden.

Gubbeen and wild sea beet pizza with sea grass

This recipe is directly inspired by the pizza cooked in Good Things Café, in Durrus, in West Cork. I have had the pleasure of doing some seaweed demonstrations at Carmel Somers' cookery school at the café, and it was during one of these that we discovered how delicious sea grass is as a topping for pizza and cheese.

pizza dough
500g strong white flour
10g dried yeast
1 teaspoon salt
350ml water
2 tablespoons olive oil

topping
olive oil, sea beet leaves, Gubbeen cheese (you can also use Durrus, or any of the other semi-soft cheeses), nutmeg and sea grass.

Combine the flour, yeast and salt in a bowl. Mix in the water, and bring together to make a dough. Knead the dough for 10 minutes. This kneading can be done in various mixers, processors or in a bread machine.

Allow the dough to rise for about 2 hours, then shape into 6 balls of dough. Preheat the oven to its hottest temperature.

Take each ball at a time and first press into a circle, then roll out thinly. Using a pizza peel, or your fingers, place on a hot oven tray. Rub the surface quickly with a little olive oil and scatter over the raw sea beet leaves (you can substitute spinach if unable to gather sea beet). Top with slices of cheese, and then sprinkle over the sea grass, and a generous grating of nutmeg.

Cook in a hot oven (as hot as it will go) for approximately 5-7 minutes. Serve straight from the oven.

You can also use this dough to make pizza swirls. Roll out the full dough into a rectangle and top with tomato sauce, or Ballymaloe Relish, cheese and seaweed. Roll up, slice, prove, and then bake for 20 minutes.

sea grass blaa

Blaa are the soft white rolls that come only from County Waterford. They are made to be eaten at breakfast-time filled with sausages and bacon or egg. This is a version mixed with sea grass.

680g strong white flour
15g dried yeast
1 teaspoon sea salt
3 tablespoons ground, dried Irish sea grass
200ml milk
130ml water
milk and flour for dusting

Mix together the flour, yeast, salt and seaweed and then add the milk and water to make a dough.

Turn out onto a board and knead for 10 minutes, or place in a food processer fitted with a dough hook, or in a bread machine with a dough setting.

Once the dough has come together, leave the dough to rest in a large bowl, covered, until it doubles in size. Leave for approximately two hours.

Punch down the bread and, using a knife, divide into six large rolls. Shape the rolls and place on an oiled baking tray. Brush lightly with a little milk, then sift over some flour. Leave to prove for another hour, until well risen.

Just before baking, sift over another dusting of flour, then place in an oven that has been preheated to 200ºC and cook for approximately 15-20 minutes.

Cool on a wire rack before splitting and filling.

Dilisk is 50 x higher in iron than spinach.

walnut and kelp bread

500g strong white flour
10g dried yeast
2-3 tablespoons finely ground kelp (kombu)
60g brown sugar
1 teaspoon salt
60g butter
300ml milk
50ml water
35g shelled walnuts

Put the flour in a large bowl along with the dried yeast, the kelp and the brown sugar. Season with a teaspoon of salt.

Heat the butter in a small saucepan, and allow it to darken slightly, into a nut brown colour. Strain the butter into the milk.

Add the milk and water to the flour mixture and knead to bring the dough together. Knead the dough for approximately 10 minutes further. At this stage you can choose to put it in a processor fitted with a dough hook, or use the dough setting on a bread machine if you have one.

Towards the end of kneading, add the waltnuts and knead until they are distributed throughout the dough.

Leave the bread to rise for approximately two hours.

Knock back the risen loaf, and carefully roll into a cylinder. It's fun to bake this loaf in a shaped tin. You could use a thin Le Creuset terrine, a flower pot, or, if you can find one, a circular loaf tin. Otherwise just use an ordinary loaf tin.

Allow the bread to prove for about another hour. Bake the loaf for approximately 35 minutes in an oven that has been preheated to 200ºC.

This bread gets better after a day or so, makes simply great toast, and is delicious served with cheese.

seaweed crackers

230g plain/spelt flour
20g rye flour
½ teaspoon salt
1 teaspoon sugar
40g butter
150ml milk
1 cup finely ground seaweed
sesame seeds / fennel seeds (optional)

Measure out the flour, salt, sugar and butter into a bowl. Rub in the butter until it resembles fine breadcrumbs.

Measure out the milk, put it into the bowl and gather the mixture together with your hands.

Knead and put it in the fridge to rest for 2 hours. Lightly grease a tray and set the oven to 180ºC.

Flour a large workspace.

Cut the dough into 6 equal-sized pieces. Press lightly on the piece of dough. Sprinkle on the seaweed and seeds and press again. Examples of combinations might be sea grass and fennel, or dried seaweed salad with sesame seeds.

Put through a pasta machine on the widest setting.

Lightly press in some more seeds or seaweed and roll again. Continue until the second last setting on the machine.

Cut into approximate squares, and place onto a tray, using a spatula to lift the delicate pieces.

Bake in the oven for approximately 10 minutes, until light brown. Cool on a wire tray.

IMPERIA
TIPO LUSSO SP150

drinks & smoothies

dilisk and rosemary lemonade

1 litre water
handful of dilisk
3 sprigs rosemary
500g sugar

lemons
sparkling water or boiling water

Make a dilisk dashi by bringing the water and dilisk slowly to the boil. Remove the seaweed the moment the water comes to the boil (consign the boiled dilisk to the compost heap).

Add the rosemary and sugar to the seaweed water and once again bring very slowly to the boil, stirring to dissolve the sugar. Take off the heat once it comes to the boil, and leave to go cold and then strain. This syrup forms the base of your drink. You can store it for a few days in the fridge and add the lemon juice and water as needed.

To make the lemonade, pour a little of the syrup into a glass. Add approximately half a lemon per glass and fill up with chilled sparkling water, or boiling water to taste. The proportions are approximately five to one water to syrup, or to taste.

rhubarb, ginger & sugar kelp cordial

700g rhubarb stems
120g ginger, grated
1 litre water
3 pieces sugar kelp
500g golden caster sugar

Clean and chop the rhubarb into short lengths. Grate the ginger, either on a grater or in a food processor. There is no need to peel the ginger first.

Place ginger and rhubarb in a large saucepan, and add 1 litre of water. Bring to the boil, and simmer for approximately 15 minutes, by which time the rhubarb will be very soft.

Press the liquid through a sieve into a bowl. Add the sugar kelp, and leave the sugar kelp marinating in the warm liquid for 1 hour. Remove the seaweed.

Place the liquid back on the heat, adding the sugar. Stir over heat until the sugar dissolves, and then bottle.

Dilute to taste with sparkling water, or use instead of the dilisk and rosemary syrup for making pink lemonade.

seaweed cures

seawater spirulina smoothie

Sea grass, which used to be called gut weed, has now started to win the name Atlantic spirulina. It shares with fresh water spirulina the fact that it is one of the oldest life forms on the planet, and that it's an algae which is nutrient dense. It also makes a great smoothie.

3 ripe bananas
2 tablespoons sea grass
350ml apple juice
350ml orange juice

Process the bananas and sea grass in a food processor or smoothie maker. Add the juices and serve.

old-fashioned carrageen cure

Carrageen is famous as a health drink for chesty invalids. It is both a natural expectorant and helps you sleep. It is also contains natural anti-biotics, and works as both an anti-viral and an anti-bacterial. Science has proven what our ancestors knew about making this drink and giving it to the unwell.

a handful of carrageen
water
lemon
honey

Place the carrageen in a small saucepan of water and bring to the boil. Simmer for about 20 minutes. Strain to make a liquid that is the basis of your drink. Dilute to taste with boiling water, and flavour with freshly squeezed lemon juice and honey.

sweet treats

Seaweed is the ultimate chameleon ingredient. If you put it with something savoury it will taste salty. But if you put it with sugar it will disappear into the background, and the sweetness of the dish will preside. It doesn't really go away though, for the umami taste hovers in the background, making the sweet taste fuller and more ambrosial.

Seaweed also adds a physical texture to a sweet dish, in the form of an unctuous jelly. Here are some recipes that complement the qualities that seaweed can give to a sweet preparation.

Seaweed controls levels of blood sugar and this in turn decreases your food cravings.

ginger jelly

1 cup dried carrageen
5 cups water
a finger of fresh ginger
rind of 1 unwaxed lemon
1 cup granulated sugar

oranges
ground cinnamon

Put the carrageen in a saucepan with the water. Grate the unpeeled ginger into the same saucepan (while you are doing this the carrageen will be re-hydrating). When you get fed up with grating, you can chop the last bit. Zest the lemon into the same pan, and lastly add the sugar.

Bring slowly to a boil, then turn the heat down and simmer very gently for 20 minutes.

Sieve the mixture into a jug and then pour the liquid into wet jelly moulds. Leave for a couple of hours to set.

Turn out and serve with orange segments in their juice, mixed with a little cinnamon.

rhubarb and carrageen not-quite-jam

We call this "not quite jam" because rhubarb isn't easy to set. Boiling the sugar beforehand is a great trick however, because this boiling is one of the things that causes a jam to stiffen. Don't worry if it's runny though. It may not be right for scones, but it's great with yogurt, ice-cream or on morning porridge.

> ***Winter carrageen is often gritty because it is picked closer to shore. It makes up for this by having better gelling qualities.***

makes approximately 5 jars

600g rhubarb
500g sugar
400ml carrageen liquid (made on a 1:5 ratio carrageen:water)
50g crystallised ginger
juice of 3 lemons

The night before you want to make the jam, slice the rhubarb into 1.5cm slices and layer in a bowl with the sugar. Left overnight, a juice will form.

When ready to make the jam, strain the fruit, adding the liquid to a large saucepan, and make sure to add any sugar residue from under the fruit. Add the carrageen liquid. Bring to the boil and boil hard for 4 minutes before adding the fruit, ginger and lemon juice. Boil again for another 4 minutes then switch off the heat. Leave the fruit to settle in the liquid for about 12 minutes, then bottle into sterilised jars. Seal while still warm.

carpaccio of pineapple with dilisk & chilli syrup

1 pineapple, skin removed
2 tablespoons rice syrup or golden syrup
pinch chilli flakes
½ teaspoon finely chopped dilisk
zest of 1 lime

Slice the pineapple as thin as you are able, whether with a sharp knife, or with a Japanese mandolin.

Heat the syrup in a small bowl, and stir in the chilli, dilisk and lime. Drizzle over the sliced pineapple.

nori granola

1 ½ cups oat flakes
½ cup sunflower seeds
½ cup cashew nuts
½ cup coconut flakes
¼ cup sesame seeds
¼ cup buckwheat
½ teaspoon cinnamon
salt
¼ cup maple syrup or honey or rice syrup
2 tablespoons coconut oil
1 teaspoon vanilla extract
¼ cup nori flakes

Combine all the ingredients in a bowl, stirring to coat everything in the sweet liquid, and to distribute the coconut oil. Place on a tray, and bake at 160ºC for about 45 minutes, watching carefully to make sure it doesn't brown. Everything should be crisp. Cool and store in an airtight jar.

Channelled wrack marks the top of the tide, serrated wrack the neap low, and forest kelp the spring low.

carrageen & vanilla milk pudding with peach melba

carrageen pudding

1 fistful of dried carrageen
900ml full-cream milk
1 vanilla pod
1 free-range egg
1 tablespoon caster sugar

Soak the carrageen in water for 10 minutes, then squeeze in your hand to remove the water and add to the milk with the vanilla pod. Bring very slowly to the boil, and keep on a low simmer for 20 minutes. Strain the milk, pressing the jelly that collects around the fronds, as well as any escaping vanilla seeds.

Slice the vanilla pod down the centre and remove the seeds along with the liquid. Add this to the strained milk.

Separate the egg and beat the yolk with the sugar. Slowly add the milk to the beaten yolk. Pour into a jug. Now, beat the white until stiff and fluffy. Add this to the milk too. Leave the pudding in the fridge until cold and set.

peach melba

4 peaches
1 cup sugar
2 cups water
1 teaspoon vanilla essence
250g raspberries
1 tablespoon peach cooking water
juice of ½ a lemon

Cut the peaches in half, lengthways and twist slightly giving you two halves. Don't worry to remove the stone yet. Dissolve the sugar in the water in a pan, and bring to the boil. Add the vanilla essence. Place the peach halves in the water, turn the heat down and simmer for about 5 minutes, turning the peaches over about half way.

Purée the raspberries with 1 tablespoon of the cooking water from the peaches. Add the juice of half a lemon, and sieve.

Remove the peaches from the sauce, stone and skin. Serve with the raspberry purée and carrageen pudding.

chocolate, hazelnut & nori ice cream

¼ cup hazelnuts
250g hazelnut chocolate paste (such as Nutella, or better still an artisan equivalent)
30g butter
500ml cream
150g sugar
salt
6 egg yolks
1 teaspoon vanilla essence
handful flaked nori
plain chocolate to serve

All land plants evolved from seaweed.

Heat the oven to 180ºC and toast the hazelnuts in the hot oven for approximately 10 minutes. Remove and place in a clean tea towel. Rub the hazelnuts between your finger and the towel, until most of the skins pop off.

Place a bowl in a saucepan of hot water to make a water bath, and gently over heat, melt to combine the hazelnut chocolate paste with the butter, beating to bring the two together.

Heat 250ml of the cream with the sugar and salt. Heat gently, making sure not to let the mixture boil.

Place the egg yolks in a bowl, and beat together. Set the bowl over a pan of boiling water on the stove, and slowly then beat in the warm cream mixture.

After a few minutes beating you will have a custard consistency.

Next beat the hazelnut chocolate mixture into the custard. The hazelnut paste should be the same temperature as the custard. Beat both together until smooth and thick. Beat in the vanilla essence.

Finally take off the heat and beat in the remaining 250ml cream. Add the handful of flaked nori. Allow to cool and then cover and leave in the fridge for a few hours until cold.

Put the mixture into an ice cream machine and chill according to the manufacturer's instructions.

Serve the ice cream with some dark melted chocolate and the toasted, skinned hazelnuts.

coconut, orange & sea spaghetti squares

Sea spaghetti has a nutty flavour that suits sweet baking, but you could also use ground kelp (kombu).

cake mix

zest of 2 oranges
10 strands dried sea spaghetti (or 2 tablespoons ground kelp)
250g self-raising flour
45g desiccated coconut
220g caster sugar
60g ground almonds
250ml buttermilk
2 eggs
150g butter

cream cheese frosting

275g cream cheese,
75g butter
90g icing sugar, sifted
nutmeg for grating

Preheat the oven to 180ºC. Grease a 23cm square cake tin, preferably with removable base.

Zest the oranges. Grind the sea spaghetti, if you are using it. Place all the cake ingredients into a food processor and process for 30 seconds.

Pour the mixture into the prepared tin and smooth the surface. Bake for approximately 50 minutes, or until a skewer, inserted into the cake, comes out clean.

Clean the food processor and this time beat together the cream cheese, butter and sieved icing sugar for the frosting.

Lift the cake out of the tin and cool. Cut into squares, but don't separate. Spread the frosting on the cake, and grate over nutmeg. Separate the individual squares, using a spatula.

Dilisk contains all the 56 minerals and trace elements necessary for human health.

nori florentines

½ cup sultanas
½ cup golden raisins
¼ cup dried morello cherries
½ cup cranberries
¼ cup flaked nori
½ cup flaked almonds
1 ½ cups organic cornflakes
⅔ cup sweetened condensed milk
250g chocolate (a mix of dark and milk)

Mix the fruit, nuts, seaweed and cornflakes together with the condensed milk in a bowl.

Line a baking sheet with parchment and spoon out circles of the mixture onto the paper. Press down slightly. Cook for 10 minutes in a moderate, 180ºC oven. Remove and once again press down to make the mixture stick together. Allow to go cold. Peel off the parchment carefully. Melt the chocolate in a bowl over a pan of hot water and either drizzle on top of the florentines, or, if you feel brave, pick them up and paint the chocolate on the underside. As the chocolate cools, mark it with a fork to make a pattern.

extreme greens

coastal foraging

Rock Samphire (a plant they valued so much in the 16th century they would tie children up by their ankles and dangle them over the cliff to get it); strong tasting scurvy grass, a Vitamin C supplement given to returning sailors; and sea beet are all common plants of coastal verges. Occasionally you'll come across sea cabbage, but you'll have to be at either the top, bottom or middle of a cliff, because these are the only places in which it grows. If you are especially lucky, you will find the purple jewel of sea kale. These are great coastal sea vegetables to seek out when on the shore.

If you are certain the area is clean and free from pollution, then shellfish are another prize for the forager. Clams of all types, cockles, limpets, mussels, and even wild oysters - sometimes native, sometimes escapees from oyster beds - are all available on the shoreline on a Spring low tide.

Left to right -
Top: Enda McEvoy cooks limpets; wild oyster
Middle:
pickled sea veg with shiitake mushrooms;
wild cabbage; wild kale
Bottom:
sea beet, rock samphire, scurvy grass

pickled coastal vegetables

cider vinegar
sea vegetables (eg sea beet, rock samphire, scurvy grass, marsh samphire)

Rinse the sea vegetables and spin dry in a salad spinner. Place in a shallow bowl and cover with cider vinegar. Leave overnight. You can re-use the vinegar. (Serve with grilled mushrooms, brown rice and a chilli vinaigrette made using the pickling vinegar).

capturing sea salt

We need salt. We like salt. And, as long as we keep to within our dietary needs, then salt is good for us. Salt has a bad name in terms of health and the reason why is the amount of salt packed into processed foods. Three-quarters of the average daily salt intake comes hidden in processed foods, with breakfast cereals, bread, cakes and biscuits being the main culprits.

But if we control our intake of it, salt is essential. Its importance is revealed in the amount of salt-derived words that pepper our language: soldier, salad, salacious, salary...

The pleasure of collecting wild salt takes on new meaning with an understanding of the elements, those indestructible substances that make us and our world. These are the raw trace elements that make salt.

We may have traded and fought over salt, but the elements, in their raw state, are things we have worshipped.

Elements begin their life in outer space. It is only through the "big bang" of a dying star, as it explodes into a supernova that enough heat is generated to create an element (gold, lead, silver, carbon etc). The supernova stars in outer space have provided all the material in our world. Salt, when captured in the wild, fuses together over 70 of these elements. So, when you eat real salt, think of it as star dust, for that is what it is.

to make sea salt

as much clean sea water as you can carry home

Boil the seawater in a large saucepan. It will reduce to almost nothing and then suddenly go white and sludgy. Watch that it doesn't burn.

When you get something close to salt, take off the heat and finish off either in a low oven or a dehydrator. Store airtight, but otherwise use as normal salt. Two large containers of water will make a season's worth of sea salt.

seaweed oven

Dig a hole in the ground. You can dig it in your garden or on the beach.

Line the hole with sand. Collect some smooth stones. You can also use bricks. Place a single layer of stones in the hole.

Make a wood fire on the stones, and burn the wood for at least two hours, until the stones are blazing hot.

After two hours, rake away the very hot wood fragments. Use a garden spade and rake to remove them. Put them in a steel bucket, or use on the BBQ.

Place a large pile of seaweed onto the hot stones, making sure to cover all of them. Use a rake to spread the seaweed. It should immediately sizzle and begin to go bright green.

The food is then placed on the seaweed. You can use lobster. If you don't want to add it live, then spear the lobster through the eyes with a large sharp knife just before cooking. Otherwise lie it on its back to cook.

Other foods you can cook include shellfish, potatoes, chicken thighs (boned and rubbed with a Cajun herb mix), ears of sweet corn, or chorizo sausages.

Cover with another very thick layer of seaweed, and then cover the whole pit with a tarpaulin, making sure no steam escapes. Leave for one hour.

After an hour, remove the food on to a hot serving plate.

Place the lobster on a board, slice down the middle, lengthways, being careful to preserve the juices.

The surprising thing is that everything seems to cook perfectly at the same time, from a simple mussel to a chicken thigh or baked potato.

hot smoking

First you will need a smoking box. You can buy these or make them. Any ventilated tin box will do, though beware biscuit tins, because their lids are too tight fitting.

For your heat source you can use a meths burner, a fire, a barbecue or the gas grill in your kitchen.

Once you have the box you will need to create the smoke. Usually this is done with wood shavings, but you can also use tea or rice.

Line your smoking vessel with kitchen foil, place a handful of the smoking medium on the foil, then put a rack on top for the food.

Once organised, you can smoke chicken, salmon or any white fish, mackerel, mussels, whelks, liver or even lamb.

Before cooking you can glaze your ingredient in a mixture of mustard and brown sugar. You can also marinate before smoking: Japanese marinades are particularly suitable. Make one with equal quantities of mirin, soy and sugar.

Timings: keep the heat moderately low, shellfish and fish fillets take about 10 minutes. Give lamb steaks about 15 minutes (use rosemary to smoke over, and in the sauce), a breast of chicken takes 15-20 minutes.

Once you've smoked your ingredient you might want to serve it with a hot sauce. A good choice is a cream sauce, made with a rich stock (fish for fish, chicken for chicken etc), reduced with some wine, and then with cream added. You can add herbs to the sauce.

Otherwise, consider tossing the smoked foods in a vinaigrette. This is especially suitable for smoked mussels.

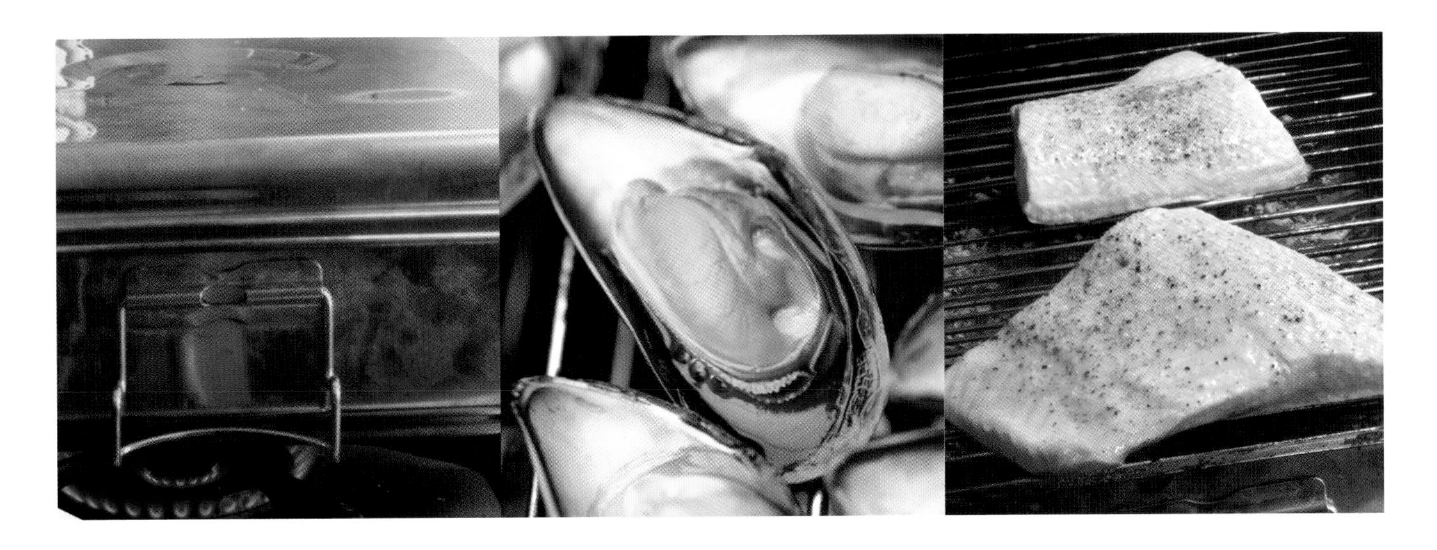

seaweed garden

Seaweed is exceptionally useful in the garden and is safe for birds, fish, worms and pollinators. You can make it into a liquid fertiliser, add it to the compost heap, simply dig it in, or dry it and use as a compost activator.

Seaweed has been used as a soil improver since the very beginning of coastal agriculture. It contains nitrogen, potassium, phosphate and magnesium. The most famous practitioners of seaweed gardening are the Aran Islanders, who for centuries have built up their soil with cartloads of seaweed.

The salt in seaweed is not present in sufficient amounts to damage crops or soil. Seaweed contains, on average, 9-12% sodium, compared to table salt which has as much as 98%. If you wish you can simply spray seaweed to remove some of the salt that resides on its fronds, or you could leave it in the rain for a few hours. Don't soak it, this will result in the loss of a lot of good surface nutrients.

Be aware also that seaweed raises soil pH, but this is seen as a benefit in most soils.

Collect seaweed that has been freshly washed up on the beach. The easiest way to use it is to dig it in before it has had time to dry.

Dig it in a spade's depth below the surface, a barrow load per square metre. You will be rewarded with increased germination, greater resistance to frost, disease and pests, and prolonged shelf life.

Seaweed has roughly the same organic content as farm manure.

seaweed tea liquid fertiliser

When applied in its natural state, seaweed needs to decompose before plants can get the benefits. But make a liquid fertiliser, and plants can immediately assimilate its goodness. Gather seaweed that has washed up on the beach. (Try to gather as many different species of seaweed as possible, they all bring slightly different nutrients). Rinse briefly with a hose to remove any salt residue. Choose a medium-sized bucket that has a lid that is not air tight, but will not blow away in the elements. A bucket with two side hinges works best. Three-quarter fill the bucket with water, and then pack in as much seaweed as the bucket can hold (it will sink and reduce in size). Stir the bucket whenever you remember. It will be ready in about four months. You'll know it's ready because it will no longer have the strong ammonia smell that characterises it while it's fermenting. Strain through a wire mesh and bottle. Dilute three to one.

extreme beauty

seaweed & skin

Skin is the largest organ in the human body, measuring on average two square metres. Skin is in a constant state of renewal, renewing itself every four weeks as new skin comes from below and then dies and becomes discarded.

Skin is different on different parts of our bodies, with the skin on our feet thirty times thicker than the skin on our eyelids.

Skin has been compared to soil* and, like soil, is a complicated layered structure that is cleverly equipped to provide a protective barrier as well as maintain temperature. Soil's layers are topsoil, subsoil and regolith, while the skin's layers are epidermis, dermis and the subcutaneous layer.

Skin plays an active role in our immune system, protecting us from disease.

Seaweed can also play an active role in helping our skin to protect us, through its anti-microbial qualities as well as its soothing, moisturising, energising properties.

* Farmacology, by Daphne Miller, MD

The study of seaweed is known as phycology.

seaweed balm

Have you anywhere on your skin that hurts? If so, put away your steroid creams, lose the antibacterials, the fungal ointments and the emollients. It's seaweeds that you need.

Seaweed is soothing, non-irritating, nourishing, and rebalancing for your skin. It acts as an anti-oxidant, locks moisture, adds vitamins, maintains a healthy skin barrier, and increases cell proliferation. Seaweed is rich in minerals and is anti-inflammatory. It revitalises your immune system, and helps to ward off bacterial attacks. Seaweed is great for your skin.

seaweed & salt curing balm

Loosely fill a litre jug with a mixture of fresh wracks & kelps
¼ cup organic sesame oil (not toasted)
3 tablespoons coarse sea salt

Process the seaweed with the oil in a food processor. Stir in the salt and then fill two small jars. The seaweed is preserved by the salt, and this balm will keep a good many months. Use for all types of skin conditions.

Minerals account for up to 80% of dry matter of seaweed.

carrageen bath and shower gel

This "soap" leaves your skin feeling clean and moisturised. The rose water is astringent and the seaweed cleans with its anti-microbial properties.

Carrageen gel is the North Atlantic equivalent of aloe vera gel. The only problem here is that it is extracted with water and, without a preservative, it will go stale easily. The trick is to sterilise everything you use in the preparation of this gel, by boiling all equipment and containers for 15 minutes in water. Pour the hot gel directly into a dark container and place in the fridge overnight. Thereafter store out of direct sunlight. It should last a week if you take these measures.

¼ cup tightly packed dry carrageen
¾ cup water
3 tablespoons rose water
a few drops of green edible food colouring

Soak the carrageen in the water for about 15 minutes, then bring to the boil and simmer on a low heat for half an hour. Strain, while still warm, through a sieve, pushing the seaweed against the sieve to extract as much juice as possible. Stir in the rose water and add some food colouring. Bottle.

Wild carrageen is red, but it is usually sold bleached white by the sun. There are many theories why this bleaching happens, but no obvious reason, other than unbleached carrageen can have a stronger taste.

medicated seaweed oil

Place 28g dried seaweed (carrageen, serrated wrack or kelp) into a Kilner jar, and pour over 500ml of oil. Grapeseed oil is light and good for perfumed preparations, sesame oil is recommended because it comes loaded with Vitamin E. Leave in direct sunlight for 2 weeks, shaking daily, then strain and store in a dark bottle.
Use in cosmetics, or as a massage oil.

banana and carrageen hair tonic

1 ripe banana
2 teaspoons seaweed oil

Mash the banana with a fork, add the carrageen oil (see left) and mash to a pulp. Smooth over your hair. Wrap some cling film over your hair, and leave for an hour. Shampoo normally. You'll be surprised how much the hair absorbs the banana oil, leaving it soft and glossy.

BATHBOMBS
HOMEMADE,
MADE WITH
SEAWEED
BATHBOMBS
HOMEMADE,
MADE WITH
SEAWEED

bath bombs

200g baking soda
100g citric acid
100g cornmeal
100g fine sea salt or epsom salts
dried seaweed flakes
scant tablespoon water
60 drops camomile oil
2½ tablespoons cooking oil
yellow food colouring (optional)
to mould: you can use baking trays, ice trays, soap moulds, or even Christmas decorations.

Mix together the dry ingredients, and squeeze out the lumps.

Mix the wet ingredients in a jar, and shake until combined.

When you are ready to make the bath bomb, slowly pour the contents of the jar into the dry ingredients, mixing all the while with your fingers.

If the mixture starts to fizz, you are adding the liquid too fast, rub the liquid into the dry powder and slow down.

When you have added all the liquid, the mixture should feel like slightly damp sand.

Press carefully into whatever mould you are using. Pack in the mixture pressing as hard as you can into the mould.

After a couple of minutes the bomb is ready to come out of the mould. This makes enough for four large bombs.

Failed bathbombs :(
Bath bombs fail because of having too little or too much water. Never fear, you can still use them. Too much water? Let them harden, then break into seaweed rocks. Too dry? Then crumble and use as seaweed sand. To make bath rocks, double the liquid. Leave the bomb overnight to fizz and expand. Next morning break into pieces.

carrageen and neroli body butter

Body butter is an easy concoction to make, since it uses only oils, and therefore will be stable and have a good shelf life. Use on dry skin.

50g shea butter
50g cocoa butter
100g carrageen oil (see medicated seaweed oil, page 177)
50g beeswax
60 drops neroli essential oil

Place the butters, carrageen oil and beeswax in a heatproof bowl, and stand over a pot of boiling water until melted. Transfer to a food processor, add the neroli oil and beat until the mixture cools and thickens. Scrape into a jar. Leave to go totally cold before putting the lid on, otherwise the condensation might cause the oil to spoil.

seaweed facemask

3 tablespoons ground seaweed
1 tablespoon water

Make a paste with the seaweed and water, and apply it to your face. Leave the mask on for 15 minutes before rinsing.

carrageen and calendula oil

Take about 30g carrageen and a large handful of calendula petals. Place in a Kilner jar, and cover with oil to fill the jar. Leave in direct sunlight for two weeks, then strain and bottle in dark bottles. Good for swelling and inflammation.

simple mineral bath

1 cup mixed dried seaweed
1 cup epsom salts

Grind the dried seaweed in a food processer. The finer the grind, the less will be left to clean up in the bath afterwards. Mix together with an equal volume of epsom salts (available from chemists). "Serve" from a bowl by the bath, using a shell to scoop the mineral bath into the warm water. Relax.

luxury mineral bath

1 cup epsom salts or coarse sea salt
½ cup dried seaweed
handful lavender flowers and/or rose petals
a few drops of grapefruit essential oil or lavender oil

Mix together and use as the recipe above.

seaweed soap with oatmeal and dandelion

This is simple if you buy a readymade soap base, available on-line and from chemists. Simply melt the soap base in a microwave or saucepan and add dried seaweed plus some chosen ingredients: here dandelion flowers for balancing and detoxifying and oatmeal for exfoliating.

Make a seaweed foot spa by adding a handful of ground seaweed to warm water.

40
30
20
10

> *Carrageen is a gentle sleep promoter. Use as a natural sedative to aid restful slumber.*

meadowsweet and wheatgerm soap bags

Meadowsweet is the original painkiller, from which aspirin was derived. So this soap is ideal for relieving tension and helping you to relax. Use a little of the soap mix in a bath to soften the water. Or use the bag as a soap itself.

You can substitute lavender flowers and add some lavender essential oil, or rose petals and rose oil, for a different bathing experience.

100g bar of soap
30g oatmeal
10g wheatgerm
2 heaped tablespoons dried meadow-sweet flowers
4 drops wheatgerm oil
large handful roughly ground seaweed

Grate the soap and mix together with all the ingredients. Bag in a muslin bag.

creamy seaweed massage oil

2 tablespoons carrageen oil
1 teaspoon cocoa butter
2 tablespoons coconut oil
smidgen of lanolin (use the top of a teaspoon to measure)
essential oil of your choice

Mix everything together either in a mini food processor, or shake well in a jar, stirring in the lanolin with a spoon if needs be.

Add essential oil according to your mood.